The Mountain
and the Chef

Emmanuel Renaut Isabelle Hintzy

The Mountain
and the Chef

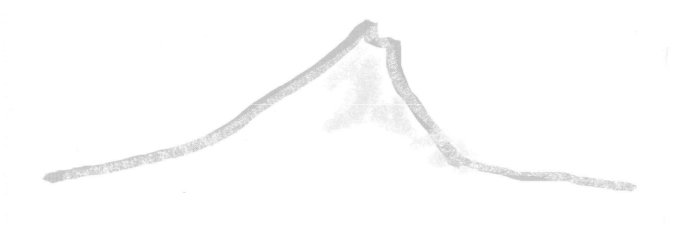

Photography by Jean-Marie del Moral

Text by Catherine de Montalembert

Aubanel

Contents

As the wind blows

The salt of the earth

The Chef

Emmanuel Renaut never sits still. He is a perfectionist; he sees everything. He talks fast, but seldom. Though born and bred in Paris, he has the remoteness and reserve of a mountain dweller. He is an avid walker, mushroom enthusiast and collector of the best vintages of Chartreuse herbal liqueur.

As a child, his parents sent him skiing in the Alps and took him to Greuze in Burgundy, where he tasted Jean Ducloux's quenelles de brochet (pike quenelles) and entrecôte marchand de vin (steak in red wine sauce). To this day, he bears the influence of this traditional chef, who was still in his kitchen at the age of 80. During one get-together, he even showed Emmanuel the recipe cards he kept jealously hidden away in his chef's hat - a true revelation!

A winner of the *Meilleur Ouvrier de France* award, Emmanuel Renaut trained at the Hôtel Crillon in Paris before working under Marc Veyrat in Annecy for seven years. In 1996, he moved to Megève to open his own restaurant, *Les Flocons de Sel*, which served as his base for inventing audacious, contemporary cuisine that pushed simplicity to its limits and led him away from the wild plants he had come to know so well. His Jerusalem artichoke with truffle became an instant classic.

By 39 years old, this prominent young chef had been permanently adopted into the mountains – and earned two Michelin stars!

The fire in the snow

Winter is a long season in the high mountains.
Under the darkened sky, the summits watch over the silent valleys.
The only things leaving the village are the river and the warm, friendly murmuring from the cafés.

Emmanuel Renaut is driving fast along the narrow, winding roads. Brooding forests line the far side – the shadowy slopes of the massif, with their pine and spruce trees blanketed with snow for the winter. A heavy snow has fallen over the past few days.

"Not a year has passed without snow since I arrived here. I even remember one unusual winter when the path to *Les Flocons* was covered in snow banks taller than a man!" he says of his restaurant, *Les Flocons de Sel*.

Today, the young Michelin-starred chef is on his way to find Jeannot, one of the region's oldest home distillers, who has set up all of his gear in front of a carpenter's workshop. Jeannot has always been a nomad, travelling from one mountain hamlet to the next. He will pass on his mantle soon enough, but for the moment, he is still watching over the secret alchemy of his still, accompanied by the folk he has picked up along the way. The rule is always to be near a spring or water supply.

It's cold out. In the morning mist, his infernal machine looks like something from a dream: part caravan, part locomotive and part Chinese dragon on the verge of breathing an intoxicating steam of fruit and wood out its smoking nostrils.

"Where's Jeannot?" asks Emmanuel, concerned. "Aha, I see him! He's over there, wearing his hat, just behind the machine. Let's just park here in case someone comes with a trailer..."

The still is already running at full steam. Belts, cylinders and pipes are making a deafening racket.

Gérard, his brother Patrick, and Gilbert have been here since daybreak. They've all brought their harvest to local carpenter Marcel's shop to transform their fermented apples, pears, plums and gentian into brandy.

It's time for the workshop's customary morning snack, but the men still take turns keeping an eye on the distiller.

Emmanuel and Gérard know each other. Gérard owns a restaurant near Annecy.

"Hey, come out and see!… 72°C! It's 72°C! … It's good! Come see, come and taste the plum!" says Gérard, handing out glasses.

"That'd kill a migraine for sure," jokes Emmanuel.

Jeannot, the keeper of secrets, is standing over the thermometer.

"It's a bit nippy - we started early this morning, and everything was frozen!" says Jeannot by way of greeting.

14

His eyes are sparkling. Jeannot is a quiet type, sparing with his words like all true mountain dwellers. Nothing seems to distract him from his still.

"Come on, Jeannot, come and have a bite to eat! Whenever we distill, everyone brings at least a couple of bottles, sometimes more!" calls Gérard.

"What do you want, a glass of white? Some red? A piece of bacon? Ah, it's nice and warm by the wood stove!" adds Patrick.

"What about you, Jeannot, a glass of white? Come on, have some ham! It's good!" Gérard shows off the cheeses he's brought: Beaufort and blue. Emmanuel savours them on a thick slice of bread.

"You know, Emmanuel, your second Michelin star really turned the region upside down - we were all so proud!

At least tell me you still love gentian, right?"

Everyone in the region knows about Emmanuel's passion for gentian. Soon, the men start talking about their tricks and trade secrets. Gérard tells the group that he treats cows by boiling gentian root with white wine and leaving it to steep.

"If you feed it to them on a slice of bread, it gets rid of their digestive problems! You shouldn't use too much, but when you take the animals up into the mountain, it can stop them having a heart attack due to the altitude change."

Before getting into the restaurant business, Gérard was a butcher. "I did that for four or five years! Then I went back to the farm when my father fell ill. That's why I know how to make cheese and understand animals."

"And what about your walnut wine, how do you make yours?" asks Emmanuel, who knows very well how strongly each man feels about his own recipe.

Gérard picks the nuts when they're still green, around 14th July, when they have not yet hardened. He cuts them into quarters, adds two or three handfuls of leaves and leaves them to soak in red wine. His brother Patrick actually adds booze! Six litres to fifteen or twenty litres of wine. In addition to leaves, his recipe includes two sticks of cinnamon and some orange peel.

"I add two vanilla pods, one star anise, a bit of juniper berry and some pepper," Emmanuel chimes in.

"Who wants coffee?" Gérard interrupts, his black hat pulled tight over his head. "A glass of red or white, anyone?"

Jeannot has come in to warm his hands by the stove while everyone troops out into the biting cold to stand around the still and taste the fresh plum brandy.

According to tradition, once the distilling is over in a few days, all of the local residents will get together with Jeannot to celebrate. In the meantime, the distiller will be housed for the night and showered with friendly invitations. It's time to go. The men exchange warm handshakes, promising to get together soon to enjoy the results of today's work under the light of the croé-zu, an oil lamp that wards off the evil eye. In times past, long evenings would be spent telling strange stories about the region and about life in the high mountain pastures, while the men whittled away and the women and children cracked walnut shells to make oil.

Winter here has always fascinated the people but has never revealed all of its secrets.

The brandy produced with Jeannot's help will see friends through their sorrows and joys until next winter.

Emmanuel would love to stop by and see his potato seller, who lives at the outskirts of the village.

"He ended up with some of my booze from last year, and I still haven't gotten it back! Every Friday, when he sells his vegetables at the market, he keeps himself warm with a swig - the customers can wait their turn!"

Emmanuel also works with another vegetable farmer, an hour's drive from the village, as well as a few grandmothers who sell him the produce from their gardens.

The sky over the mountains is fresh and blue.

Emmanuel's mobile phone rings:

"Hello, hello, yes, yes, I'm coming! I'll stop by and pick you up - we'll have lunch! Tschüss!"

It was Kristine, his wife. They met in London when they were both working at Claridge's Hotel. Kristine is German, so the family always wraps up their short phone calls with tschüss.

"Every Wednesday we go sledging, just for the children! I work like crazy, but that one day is for us. It's harder during high season. In fact, I haven't taken a day off since 1st December!"

If it's nice on Wednesday, the whole family will eat lunch on the terrace of a little restaurant overlooking Mont-d'Arbois, as they often do. The menu is unique, and varies depending on the chef's mood. Locals and tourists alike never tire of the landscape standing before the chapel that overlooks the terrace.

On the way back, Emmanuel even remembers to stop in at the Refuge du Boulanger. He'll pick up pains au chocolat, croix-de-Savoie and Saint-Genix brioches to enjoy with the family.

"The dough is alive; it never takes the same shape. Did you know that a hint of olive oil in a white bread helps to keep it soft a little bit longer?"

Rémy Coste, the baker, is a friend of Emmanuel's. Each of them has been named the accolade of *Meilleur Ouvrier de France* (Best Worker of France) and they share a strict sense of work well done. Rémy opened his first bakery six years ago.

It's on the corner, right near *Les Flocons de Sel*. The oven and kneading machine are in full view of passers-by and bathed in sunlight, which is rare for a baker's kitchen. The staff listen to music as they work, and the corn flour smells delicious.

Customers peek in as they wait their turn, checking on how the bread is that day and picking up Chef's Baguettes, Torchon, Aromatic and Rustic loaves as though collecting precious treasure.

Children stare wide-eyed at an apprentice conscientiously forming the dough. During Tasting Week, Rémy hosts groups of ten or twelve children at a time. They learn to knead, cut, form, bake and taste bread - and leave grinning from ear to ear wearing their chef's hat and carrying the little loaves they've baked themselves.

"They're my future customers!" says Rémy.

He has worked with Emmanuel right from the start. It's Rémy who supplies the small pies the chef serves in his restaurant. Emmanuel toasts them slightly and serves them with his vegetable soup.

Even though there are three other Refuges du Boulanger in far-flung corners of the valley, all of the bread is baked here. "I can't be everywhere, but I see everything! What's being kneaded, what's coming out of the oven... I'd rather worry about deliveries - and God knows we deliver all day long! - than have any doubts on the quality of my bread."

Rémy tells us about his craft, which unfortunately is slowly disappearing, and how hard it is to find people who are passionate about it. Apprentices who join him learn the art of making high-quality bread baked in a wood-burning oven.

Right now, he has five young apprentices: three work the night shift, and two cover the afternoon. Samuel arrived at the start of the winter season and will stay until September. After that, he'll see.

Since the dawn of time, bread has required a great deal of work and attention, and constant daily care. "In this big mountain village," Rémy explains, "quantities are hard to predict because of the seasons. There are peaks, especially in the winter. Production can increase twenty-fold or fall off just as much! During the busy season, we might go through the bread-making process as many as fifteen times."

The leaven is prepared twice a day: the night team needs to start it at midnight for the next day's batch of bread. The stack of flour bags against the wall is constantly replenished. The baker is very demanding in his choice of ingredients, ranging from traditional flour to wholemeal, spelt, corn and chestnut flours.

"The dough is alive; it never takes the same shape. Did you know that a hint of olive oil in a white bread helps to keep it soft a little bit longer?"

Rémy greets a few customers. It's time to go already; they're waiting for him in another one of his bakeries where pastries are made.

Emmanuel is very interested in sugar, which is rather unusual for a chef.

"Rémy is always telling me that chocolate doesn't mix well with flour - it gets everywhere!" he quips, bustling around his kitchen after the service is over.

He's had to refine his efforts. That was how he perfected his Chocolate Balloon Flambéed with Gentian, the centrepiece of the dessert menu at *Les Flocons de Sel*.

"You blow up a rubber balloon, just like when you were a kid. Then you pour the warmed chocolate over it. I saw it done a long time ago - at Easter, we used them to make chocolate nests. But be careful: the balloon can explode, and it's not funny when that happens! At least, the guy who gets a faceful doesn't think so!

Potato and Fontina Fondue

Serves 4 to 6

500 g firm-fleshed potatoes
(Linzer Delikatess, BF15,
Ratte varieties)
25 cl whipping cream
150 g fontina
a sprinkling of truffle flakes
(optional)
salt

cream siphon
2 chargers
1 sieve

Wash the potatoes but leave them peeled. Simmer in salted water for about twenty minutes.

Warm up the cream and add the grated fontina.

Drain and peel the potatoes, then mash them through the sieve. Combine this purée with the fontina cream and season to taste.

Pour the mixture into the siphon. Insert both chargers and shake vigorously – this will produce a lighter fondue. Set aside in a bain-marie.

Serve in bowls as a side dish or starter, garnished with truffle flakes.

Wine pairing: White Côtes du Jura, Les Murgers 2003
(Domaine Voorhuis-Henquet)

Reblochon Spring Rolls

Serves 4

1 round Reblochon
    (farmhouse or
    shop-bought)
8 spring roll pastry sheets
1 litre oil
a few mint and/or
    lettuce leaves

Here is a simple dish to enjoy with friends over a drink.

Scrape the Reblochon rind but do not remove it (except for the label). Cut the cheese into 8 rectangles. Wrap each piece of cheese in a spring roll pastry sheet and shape into rolls, sealing the edges with water using a brush.

Just before serving, deep-fry the spring rolls for 2 minutes in very hot oil (170°C). Dry with a paper towel and serve them with a few mint and lettuce leaves.

Wine pairing: Chignin-Bergeron 2005 (Domaine Denis & Didier Berthollier)

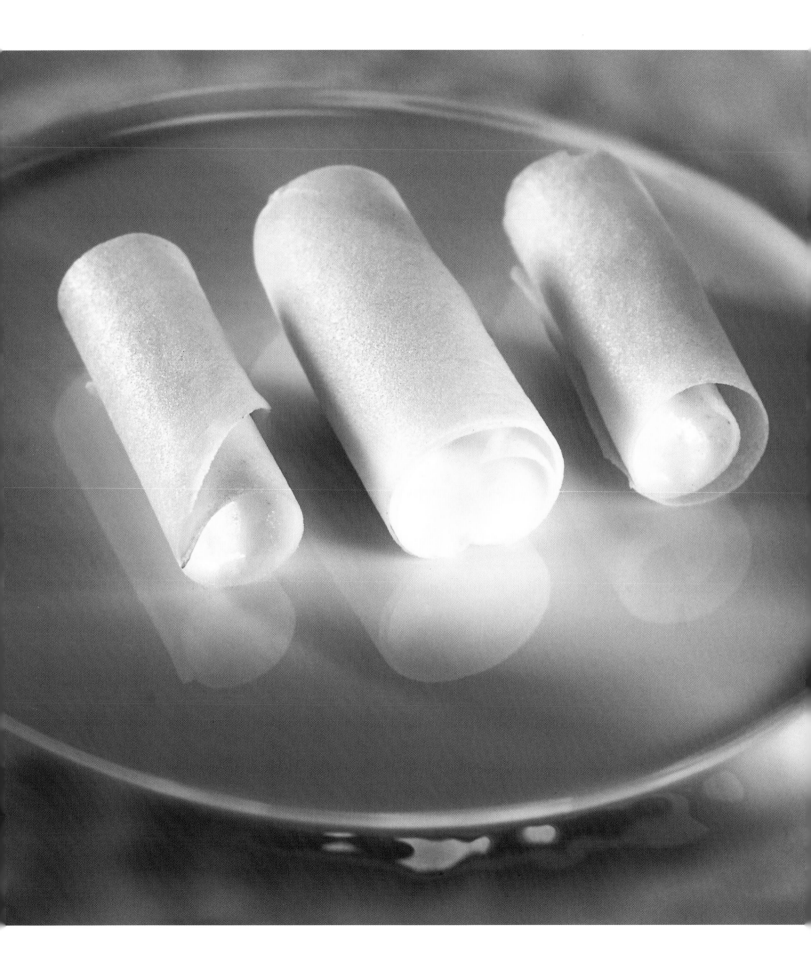

Arthaz Jerusalem Artichoke, Cardoons in Butter Broth and Truffle

Serves 8

300 g cardoons
2 tablespoons olive oil
1 bouquet garni
½ lemon
1 kg Jerusalem artichokes
30 g black truffle
    (Melanosporum)
salt, pepper

For the broth
25 cl chicken stock
1 teaspoon cloves
150 g butter
10 cl truffle juice

Clean and slice the cardoons, then sauté in olive oil for several minutes. Add the bouquet garni, pepper, salt and a few drops of lemon juice. Cover with water and cook for approximately 30 minutes, until the cardoons are tender: prick with a knife to check when they are done. Leave them in their cooking juices to cool.

Clean and thinly slice the Jerusalem artichokes. Steam for 1 to 2 minutes. Arrange 12-cm rounds in an overlapping circle over the plastic wrap.

Next, prepare the garnish: dice the cooked cardoons and the remaining Jerusalem artichokes, season to taste with salt and pepper and add half the grated truffle.

Place a generous scoop of the mixture in the centre of the circle arrangement. Use the plastic wrap to form a sealed pouch. Return to the steamer to keep warm.

Prepare the sauce: reduce the chicken stock by half and let the cloves steep. Strain the stock, then chop the butter into pieces and whisk it into the mixture.

Add the truffle juice at the last moment, and emulsify using a whisk.
Pour into soup bowls over the Jerusalem artichoke cakes, removed from their plastic wrap, with the remainder of the grated truffle.

If necessary, artichokes can be substituted for the cardoons.

Wine pairing: Meursault Tête de Murger 2002 (Domaine P. Javillier)

Pure White Pike
with Hibiscus

Serves 4

For the pike stuffing
300 g raw pike flesh
    (to be prepared by
    your fishmonger)
12 g salt
12 g caster sugar
2 eggs
70 g whipping cream
1 cl armagnac
60 g butter
4 thin slices sandwich
    bread (2 mm thick)
50 g clarified butter*

For the sauce
25 cl vegetable stock
1 tablespoon - hibiscus
50 g butter

Prepare the stuffing: blend the pike with the salt and the sugar. Add the eggs, whipping cream, armagnac and warm, melted butter. Mash through the sieve and pack into a mould or rectangular dish. Wait two minutes for the stuffing to get warm. Strain.

Gently spread the stuffing out on the work surface, using a pastry cutter to form it into a square. Place it on a plate, then steam for 15 minutes over simmering water (80°C). Leave to cool.

Cut rectangles of bread and stuffing of the same size. Place the stuffing on the bread and brown it in a non-stick pan using clarified butter*. Set aside in a warm oven (90°C).

For the sauce: reduce the vegetable stock by half and steep the hibiscus in it. Strain the resulting mixture. Dice the butter and whisk it in, then season to taste.

Arrange the toasted hors d'œuvre on a plate and serve with the sauce.

Wine pairing: Chablis 1er Cru Montée de Tonnerre 2001
(Domaine François Raveneau)

Tartlets with Blood Sausage and Apples

Makes 8 tartlets

500 g Reinette apples
150 g blood sausage
several fennel seeds
sea salt

For the dough
100 g butter
8 g salt
45 g icing sugar
1 egg
2 egg yolks
250 g flour

16 tartlet moulds

Prepare the dough: cream the butter* with the salt, sugar, whole egg and two egg yolks (thoroughly beaten), then mix the flour in gently. Cover with a cloth and refrigerate for 15 minutes.

Roll out the dough very thinly and press into the moulds (this is a very fragile dough so only small moulds should be used). Cover each tartlet with an identical mould and set aside in the refrigerator.

Bake the tartlets for 10 to 12 minutes at 150°C, leaving the larger mould on top and removing it halfway through.

Prepare the apple sauce: peel, core and dice the apples, then steam them for approximately 20 minutes. Mash the steamed apple through the sieve. Keep the apple sauce warm.

Remove the skin from the blood sausage and cut it into evenly-sized cubes. Collect the sausage trimmings and arrange them in the bottom of the tartlets; cover with warm apple sauce and sausage cubes.

Return the tartlets briefly to the oven at 150°C to warm them.

Just before serving, sprinkle the tartlets with a few grains of coarse sea salt and fennel seeds.

Wine pairing: Jacquesson Cuvée no. 730 Champagne

Endive, **Arnaz** Bacon and Orange Salt **Tarts**

Serves 4

6 endives
50 g + 25 g butter
15 g salt
1 or 2 tablespoons
    caster sugar
½ lemon
5 juniper berries
100 g puff pastry
    (see recipe page 216)
4 thick slices cooked
    Arnaz bacon

For the orange salt
zest of 2 oranges
30 cl syrup (150 g caster
    sugar, 15 cl water)
20 g sea salt

4 small pie tins

Prepare the orange salt: blanch the orange zest by dipping it three times in boiling water, then candy it slightly with the syrup (see recipe page 62 for cooking syrup). Once the orange zest is transparent, drain it and bake in a warm oven (80°C) for 1 hour on waxed paper. Check that the zest is crunchy, then mix with the sea salt. Mash the mixture through the sieve.

Wash and dry the endives, then soak them for several minutes in a covered pot with 50 g of butter, the salt, the sugar, a few drops of lemon juice and the juniper berries. Cook them in a saucepan of boiling water for about half an hour (or 10-15 minutes in a pressure cooker).

Leave to cool, then dry using a cloth. Cut the endives in half lengthwise and fry in the remaining butter to caramelize them slightly. Arrange 3 endive halves in each pie tin and cover with a thin layer of puff pastry. Finish baking in the oven at 240°C for about ten minutes: the crust should be well browned.

Finally, flip the tart over like an upside-down cake and serve immediately with the bacon slices and orange salt powder.
It can be served alone or as a side dish with fish or meat.

Arnaz bacon is a fatty bacon from farmhouse pigs raised in the village of Arnaz, in the Aosta Valley, which is salted and smoked with herbs and spices: juniper berries, pepper, thyme, rosemary, etc.

Wine pairing: Roussette de Savoie 2003 (Domaine Michel Grisard)

Crunchy Toast with Vegetable Soup

Serves 4

1 loaf hazelnut or
    bacon bread
1 piece tomme

For the soup
1 leek
2 carrots
1 celery root
1 potato
50 g butter
1 piece bacon
salt

This is a simple, rustic recipe.
The most important thing is to find good, flavourful vegetables.

Prepare the country soup: cut all the vegetables into small pieces, "rustic-style". Sweat them with butter in a saucepan, then cover them generously with water. Add the bacon and simmer gently in water for 1 hour, lid on, adding water if necessary. Remove the bacon halfway through cooking and season to taste.

For the crunchy toast: cut several-day-old bread into very thin (2 mm) slices, then arrange them between two sheets of greaseproof paper. Bake for 30 minutes on medium heat (150°C), then keep warm until it is time to serve the soup.

Serve the soup with the slices of toast and a piece of tomme cheese.

Macaroni, Truffle and Mountain Cheese Risotto

Serves 4

100 g macaroni
10 cl whipping cream
30 g mascarpone
40 g grated mountain cheese
(mixture of abondance,
Swiss gruyère
and tomme)
30 g truffle

Cook the macaroni for 5 minutes in plenty of salted, boiling water. Drain and leave to cool.

Reduce the whipping cream by one third and add the macaroni, leaving the saucepan over the heat and stirring well to heat the pasta. Add the grated cheese, mascarpone and diced truffle.

The truffle, if making for children for example, can be replaced with cubes of boiled ham.

Wine pairing: Vin Jaune 1988 (Domaine Puffeney)

Tart Soufflée with Chartreuse

Serves 6

For the shortcrust pastry
250 g flour
100 g butter
4 egg yolks
1 egg white
95 g icing sugar
1.5 g baking powder

For the Chartreuse jelly
150 g caster sugar
6 g agar
10 cl Chartreuse for cooking, 140 proof

For the Chiboust
8 egg yolks
50 g caster sugar
20 g confectioner's cream powder or flour
25 cl milk
25 g double cream
4 sheets gelatine

For the meringue
150 g caster sugar
8 egg whites

10 cl Chartreuse elixir
brown sugar

6 rings (or tartlet tins), 10 cm in diameter
6 rings, 9 cm in diameter and 2 cm high

For the tart crust: make a shortcrust pastry using all of the ingredients (set aside a little egg yolk for glazing). Cut out circles 10 cm in diameter. Line the tart crusts with waxed paper, then set a weight on top (such as baking beans). Bake the tart crusts for about twenty minutes in an oven preheated to 150°C.
Remove the weight and the waxed paper. Glaze* the tart crusts using a pastry brush (mix a bit of egg yolk with a pinch of salt and a few drops of water), then return to the oven for 5 minutes.

For the Chiboust: mix the egg yolks with the sugar and confectioner's cream powder. Pour in the boiling milk. Return to the saucepan and cook for 5 minutes over a low heat, whisking like a confectioner's custard. Add the double cream and the gelatine, previously softened in a bain-marie. Keep warm.

For the meringue: beat the egg whites until they form stiff peaks. Cook the sugar with 50 cl of water to 121°C. Pour the resulting syrup over the egg whites, beating constantly.

Mix the Chiboust with the Chartreuse elixir and the warm meringue. Form the mixture into circles 9 cm in diameter and place in the freezer.

For the Chartreuse jelly: boil 40 cl of water with the sugar. Add the agar, return to a boil, stir and then add the Chartreuse.

Pour ½ cm of jelly into the tart crusts. Cover with Chiboust and bake for 10 minutes at 150°C. Sprinkle with brown sugar and place briefly under the grill to caramelize the sugar.

Serve with the liqueurs.

Wine pairing: Tasting of Green Chartreuse VEP and Yellow Chartreuse Tarragona 1965

Chocolate Balloons
with Gentian Flambée

Serves 4

1 kg dark chocolate
1 tablespoon syrup
    (see recipe page 158)
20 cl gentian

For the chocolate mixture
200 g dark chocolate
150 g butter
3 eggs
40 g sugar
50 g flour
5 cl milk
50 g cream

pastry thermometer
4 rubber balloons
4 pastry rings
    (12 cm, stainless steel)
waxed paper

Melt the chocolate in a bain-marie, monitoring the temperature closely: heat to 55-58°C, cool down to 28°C (it should have the consistency of an ointment), then warm up to 32°C.
This procedure helps the chocolate to crystallize more effectively, making it glossy and crunchy.

Blow up the balloons to a diameter of approximately 12 cm. Dip them halfway into the chocolate, then shake them slightly until they are covered with a thin shell. Turn them upside-down over a saucepan and leave to cool.

Make the liquid mixture: melt the 200 g of chocolate with the butter. Beat the eggs with the sugar and flour until they turn a pale yellow colour.
Boil the milk with the cream. Pour in the melted chocolate and add the liquid to the egg/flour/sugar mixture.

Line the stainless steel rings with waxed paper and fill them with the mixture. Set aside in the refrigerator.

Just before serving, bake the rings in a hot oven (220°C) for 6 to 10 minutes: the mixture should be crunchy on the outside but remain runny in the centre.

Remove, still warm, from the rings onto a plate.

Pop the balloons. The chocolate shells should come off easily: remove them and place them over the four circles of baked chocolate with liquid centres.

Just before serving, boil 20 cl of water with the syrup. Add the gentian, flambé and pour over the chocolate shells, which will melt away.

Wine pairing: Maury Cuvée Agnès 1998 (Domaine de la Coume du Roy)

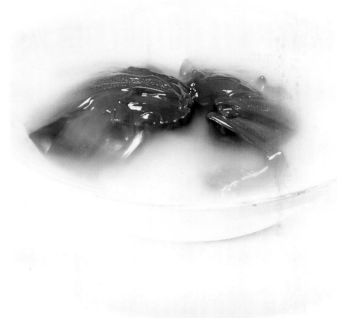

The Garden, the Mountains and Herbal Tea

The plants that we use for herbal teas are grown in our garden, half a mile away from the restaurant, which provides all of our herbs: sage, lemon balm, mint, verbena, lovage, southernwood, chartreuse, rue, parsley, chervil, marigolds, chives, strawberries, raspberries and more.

We collect linden and rose hips in the mountains.

After picking the herbs, we strip the leaves off and dry them for several days on sheets of newspaper in a well-ventilated attic room, away from the light, before using them. Then we select them depending on their purpose (tonic infusion, liqueur, etc.) and add jasmine flowers, liquorice, orange blossoms or other ingredients.

Liqueur Bonbons

**Makes about fifty
liqueur bonbons**

8 cl brandy or liqueur
250 g caster sugar
250 g corn starch

automatic piston funnel
cork
pastry thermometer

Pour the starch onto a baking sheet in a 50°C oven to warm it, then sift it into a box 3 to 4 cm deep. Dig a cork into the starch to form hollows to pour the syrup into.

Cook the sugar with 10 cl of water to 115°C. Dip the bottom of the saucepan in cold water to stop the syrup cooking, then add the alcohol and stir gently to obtain a liquid with an even consistency.

Use an (automatic piston) funnel to fill each hollow with syrup. Cover with starch, sprinkling it over the surface using a colander. Set the box aside in a warm place (the airing cupboard or a warm baking sheet in an oven that has been turned off) for 6 hours.

Remove each bonbon using a fork, brushing off excess starch with a pastry brush.
Enjoy the bonbons plain or dipped in melted chocolate.

Like water
from a spring

The Tour de France route always passes close by... The tunnel is under construction.
The Aiguilles d'Arves rise up towards the heavens.
One of them, at over 3,000 metres altitude, looks like the head of a cat.

Along the road that follows the torrent of glacier melt, the mountain pastures flush with the first greens of a fickle spring. The air is cool. The torrent of water has spent centuries digging out potholes, forming whirlpools and sculpting waterfalls. A white-throated dipper has just landed on a rock in the middle of the river. Just a few days ago, the last snow still lay over the pastures.

Nestled in the heart of this high valley in the Savoie, near the Col de la Croix-de-Fer, the Vallée des Arves cheese cooperative produces soft, creamy Beaufort cheese with its cooked, pressed curd and fruity flavour. The little shop stands next to the production workshop and the cellars.

The dairy shopkeeper sells mountain butter, crozets, bags of walnuts and every form of Beaufort imaginable! "We usually sell all our Beaufort in eight months. We can't keep enough to age it longer! But the real connoisseurs order ahead."

The cheesemaker arrives, dressed in white from head to toe: he's the one who gives the cheese its soul.

Beaufort is symbolic of the pastoral agricultural system of the high mountains. The herds move around with the changing seasons, ranging as high as 2,500 metres. The cows (Tarine and Abondance breeds), fed exclusively on hay and grazed pastures, produce the precious high-altitude milk. Beaufort alone takes up almost all of the hectares of pastureland in the Savoie. Seven cooperatives in the region are responsible for producing, maturing and selling the cheese, thanks to the help of more than five hundred farmers.

"Our cooperative collects the milk from forty of the farmers, spread out among five villages, and we produce five thousand wheels of cheese a year. I see you've noticed our trophies - they are given to winners of contests between cooperatives. In 2003, we won the gold medal at the *Concours Général Agricole*! Our most recent award is from 2004."

We start work early in the production workshop, every morning of every day! The cows don't care if it's Sunday. The sour smell of the whey floats in the air, a reminder of the time when each village had its own *fruitière* where butter and cheese were produced.

The milk collected from the day's milking arrives in cans, transported mechanically from the large copper tanks that have replaced the cauldrons used in days gone by. The workshop produces up to twenty-four wheels at a time, each weighing some forty kilos. Next, the milk is heated to the ideal temperature (33°C) for natural, traditional rennet - produced from the abomasum of grown calves - to be added. Once the milk becomes firm and "curdles," it is cut into pieces the size of grains of rice. It is heated for another half hour, then stirred over the heat to ensure that the whey is completely drained.

The cheese maker is firmly at the helm. He is the one who uses his expert touch to adjust the flavour of the cheese. That touch has a hand in every factor from the size of the tanks to the reaction of the milk. When he feels that the texture is right, he removes the mass of curds from the tanks and places it in a cloth bag within a hoop made of beechwood, giving the Beaufort its distinctive concave sides. The cheese will then be pressed for twenty-four hours.

Once the cheese is produced, it is turned for the first time and the famous blue casein label is stencilled on as a guarantee of the AOC status of the Beaufort wheel. It is turned twice more. The wheels are left in the cold for one day and one night. Next, the still-fragile cheese is plunged into a vat of brine for the first round of salting.

After the first three days, the wheels of cheese are sent to the cellars, where they will be salted and scraped twice a week. This is when the cellar master takes over from the cheese maker. He or she is responsible for developing the cheese's subtle flavours over five to ten months in the naturally-ventilated underground cellars. The wheels are arranged by age on shelves made of untreated oak: new, young and ripe. Those that have been aged for the longest - at least three years - are moved into a cooler cellar, redolent with strong, bitter aromas, to make way for the new arrivals.

"We also have a lot of direct retail outlets, both high-quality wholesalers and small-scale cheese ripeners who reserve their wheel in advance."

"I didn't see where the salt is stored," hints Emmanuel.

"One day I'll have to take you to see the milking out in the pastures! The farm belongs to my friend Joseph's parents. Watching the milking there is a real pleasure! I've already introduced Joseph to Michel Rostang, who has a restaurant in Paris but is originally from Grenoble. He shares my passion for the Grande Chartreuse monastery."

"The kitchen there is fantastic! Especially the marble slab right in the middle. No one gets in there. I'm truly touched by their trust in me. Actually, I think today is the day of their picnic! Once a year, the monks get a day off. They live at 1,500 metres altitude and mostly eat the vegetables from their own garden, but today they'll spend the whole day in the mountains with a hearty snack!"

"And they know how much I love Chartreuse liqueur, too. I've been collecting it for about ten years. The elixir is the base for the recipe. The Chartreuse monks figured that if they put all the plants in, it would cure anything! The recipe has always been a secret. I had the incredible privilege of going into the room where all the plants are stored. The hundred and thirty herbs and spices used in preparing Chartreuse are kept in closed wooden chests. It's such a shame that you can't take the smells home with you - they're incredible! The 1605 batch reminds me of freshly cut grass, a bit like the smell in the hay loft! And there's no comparison between the yellow and the green, they don't have the same alcohol content and they're not made with the same spices. But the amount of sugar is exactly the same!"

After the cheese is produced, it is turned for the first time and the famous blue casein label is stenciled on as a guarantee of the AOC status of the Beaufort wheel. It is turned twice more. The wheels are left in the cold for one day and one night. Next, the still-fragile cheese is plunged into a vat of brine for the first round of salting.

A corridor separates the laboratory from the boat shed.

Éric Jacquier always dreamed of having his boats out of the elements.

He designed the shed himself, a design straight out of a James Bond film,

built of aluminum to keep it light but sturdy.

The boat slides slowly along the track down to the dark water and

slips away from the wooded slopes surrounding the lake.

Emmanuel's phone rings: "Ah, I can't tomorrow. I'm going fishing! But I noticed a couple of nice water jugs in your window. I'll take them!... That was my friend the antique dealer," he says after hanging up. "She's the one that helped me find *Flocons* and the furniture in it. I call her Granny - but it's an affectionate nickname!"

Better call the Chamonix weather line... Monsieur Jacquier, you're back already? Yes, I know, the weather is awful! What are you sending me tomorrow? Crayfish? And char? There won't be enough fish for everyone? Okay, then send me twenty kilos of crayfish and some perfect feras!"
Emmanuel is worried about the lake fisher. Fishing is hard in this corner of Lake Geneva. The first time they talked, Éric Jacquier told him:
"I never supply chefs who don't come fishing with me!"
So Emmanuel joins him sometimes on his early-morning forays out on the deep blue lake.
"Alright, let's get going!... There's nothing in Evian, except the water, of course."

Nathalie, the fisherman's wife, is already hard at work at the fishery scaling the feras. Emmanuel asks if there's any pike left.

Nathalie has already promised the last ten kilos from this morning to a customer who came in yesterday wanting fera too! And there won't be enough fera for everyone.
Emmanuel offers to give up his share.
"But where's the new boat? And where's the old one?"
"It's in Dieppe," answers Éric Jacquier, who's just arrived with the coffee. "I'm going to put it up for sale."

But fishing is his life! "I started fishing to finance my design studies at a school in Vevey, Switzerland, and to cover transportation and food. But over the summer, even when I worked every day starting at three in the morning, I couldn't bring in enough money to cover my expenses. Once I tasted freedom, I couldn't go back!

If I'm too far away from the lake, I'm miserable. I even did my military service with the Alpine Huntsmen in Annecy, where I was the only 'alpine fisher'." I had the whole battalion up in arms! And then I met Nathalie and we fell in love. I had just taken up fishing again, and she was a banker; she handled money all day long! It used to give me a headache in the evening. Our first child, Mathilde, was born soon after, and Nathalie generously chose to stop working to come take care of the baby - and the fish!

Come on, Emmanuel, let's go pull up the nets! Just have to find you some boots... will a 43 fit? I'm always amazed to find a chef who's willing to join in. You can't even find one in a hundred - more like one in a thousand!"

A corridor separates the laboratory from the boat shed. Éric Jacquier had always dreamed of having his boats out of the elements. He designed the shed himself, a design straight out of a James Bond film, built of aluminium to keep it light but sturdy. The boat slides slowly along the track down to the dark water and slips away from the wooded slopes surrounding the lake. The on-board computer detects the motion of schools of fish and flags up the location of the nets. Eric has been plying his trade for almost twenty years now, and he has seen some serious storms out on the lake. He's fought through water, wind and snow. And yet somehow, when he fishes on the ocean with his colleagues from the Atlantic and the Mediterranean, they tease him by calling him a "freshwater fisherman"! When they take their turn visiting him for a few days' skiing and to see his facilities, they're in shock!

By 1500 or so, the Jacquier family was already selling fish at the Evian market. Eric's grandfather and his father were fishermen; his father was a cabinetmaker as well, and later sold furniture. Like many people, he had two trades: one to put food on the table, and one that was his passion. As for the grandfather, he always refused to do anything else, even during the biggest fishing crises. Eric has always thought that if one day, one of his three children wanted to take up the trade, they would have to have the skills and the strength. Fishing wears you down, after all!"

That's why he's always improving his tools. He worked with a fellow from a company in Brittany, which produces equipment for pulling in bass fishing lines, to adapt the winch system used for ocean nets to the lake. The two men combined their ideas and experience to reinvent a patented system. Eric is betting that all the boats on the lake will be using it within two years, even though he still comes across as a bit eccentric for now.

He scans the sky. The lake won't warm up anytime soon with the cold weather and snow melt... And if today is any sign, spring is definitely taking its time.

Goosanders flock together on the water's surface. These lake birds, a sort of threatening, black and white seagull, mingle with the wild ducks, cormorants and gulls. The voracious goosanders are not content just to eat the bait. Instead, they rush over when the nets are brought in, flying along the surface of the water. Then, a dozen metres before the net appears, they dive underwater to pull the fish out with their teeth! "This is crazy! There never used to be so many pests!" he protests, pulling in the net.

"It takes two successive spawning seasons to have one generation of perch. It's a well-known phenomenon. If a perch is the only one of its generation, it will take two and a half or even three years to become an adult. It has just enough to survive, but not enough to grow. That leads to these super generations of perch that turn cannibal. They eat the little ones as soon as their own eggs hatch. So the whole thing breaks down! And just when you think there's absolutely nothing left... a new generation arrives! Once, we thought we had eaten the last perch in the lake. Two years later, our hands were bleeding from pulling so many fish out of the nets! The hard part is explaining all these things to the customer - but that's another kettle of fish!

There's so much choice today in supermarkets. When monkfish are in season, that's exactly when the customer doesn't want any. And then as soon as the season ends, he changes his mind! Look at that: today, we've got a dozen trout. That's six or seven kilos... And we hadn't seen a single trout in a very long time before now! Fishing is like that.

Thirty years ago, the Arctic char had all but disappeared. We went to find them elsewhere so that they could crossbreed with the ones in Lake Geneva. It takes maybe fifty years for everything to return to scratch."

The boat turns toward the crayfish pots. Eric picks up the traps. "This isn't our culture at all! But we imitated the way fishermen in Brittany and Charente fish for lobster and shrimp. Oh, all sorts of new things are created when lake fishers and sea fishers get together!"

Emmanuel leaves with the crates Nathalie prepared. Eric promises his wife that he'll take her to *Flocons* one of these nights. The next time they go fishing, Emmanuel will bring his daughters. Today, though, it's the littlest one, Clément, who's waiting for him to water the herbs in the garden. "We have a little of everything. I pick it fresh every morning! Chives, mint, lemon balm, and the onions are about to flower. I'll use them to decorate the restaurant. Onion flowers - how marvellous is that!"

Arctic Char from Lake Geneva, Blackcurrant Juice and Green Tea

Serves 4

1 Arctic char, 1.5 kg (the
   finest fish in the world)
50 g butter
200 g blackcurrants
1 pinch Matcha tea
salt
sugar

For the char broth
10 cl vegetable stock
1 shallot
100 g butter
½ lemon
salt, pepper

For the char broth: reduce the vegetable stock by half with the finely chopped shallot. Strain. Add the butter in small pieces while whisking. Season with salt, a pinch of sugar and a few drops of lemon juice. Set aside in a warm place.

For the blackcurrant juice: cook the blackcurrant berries for a few minutes, then mash and strain them. Set aside the resulting coulis.

Prepare the fish: remove and clean the fillets. Season them and fry in butter over a low heat, skin side down, taking care to leave the flesh pink. Remove the fillets from the pan and flip them over onto a plate; leave to rest for several minutes: they will continue to cook while you wait.

Serve the fillets with the char broth, a few drops of blackcurrant juice and a sprinkling of green tea powder.

Matcha tea is powdered green tea used in the traditional Japanese tea ceremony. Its smell of lake fish and fishing nets is perfect for this recipe.

Wine pairing: Chignin-Bergeron Vieilles Vignes 2005
(Domaine François Quénard)

Lake-Caught Fera, Capers and Quinoa

Serves 4

2 large fera fillets
100 g quinoa grains
1 teaspoon small capers
1 tablespoon finely
    chopped chives
3 quarters of 1 lemon
3 mint leaves
2 cl hazelnut oil
several croutons
50 g butter

Cut the fillets in half, without removing the skin, and check for bones.

Cook the quinoa in salted, boiling water for 20 minutes. Drain and set aside. Cut the capers into small pieces, mix them with the finely chopped chives and mint and the diced lemon.

In a frying pan, melt the butter over a low heat until it browns, then fry the fillets with the skin down for 3 to 4 minutes. When the skin is crunchy, flip the fillets, then set them aside on a tray to keep warm.

Warm up the quinoa with the hazelnut oil, add the caper/herb mixture and season to taste.

Just before serving, place the fera fillets very briefly under the grill. Serve with the quinoa and a few browned croutons.

Wine pairing: La Grande Côte 2000 White Sancerre
(Domaine François Cotat)

Perch Meunière
with Lemon Salt

Serves 4

350 g perch fillets
zest of 2 lemons
200 g caster sugar
1 tablespoon flour
5 cl spirit vinegar
5 cl white wine
150 g butter
sea salt
    or fine sea salt

Prepare the fillets without removing the skin (do not rinse them, so as not to ruin the flavour) and check that no bones remain.

Season with table salt and lightly flour the skin side. Set aside.

For the lemon salt: blanch the lemon zest three times in succession. Drain the zest, then cook for several minutes in 40 cl of water with the sugar. When it turns transparent, dry in a 100°C oven for 1 to 1½ hours; it should be dry and brittle. Grind to obtain a powder. Weigh it and combine with an equal quantity of coarse sea salt.

For the sauce: reduce the vinegar with the white wine by half. Add the butter in small pieces with 1 teaspoon of water, whisking constantly. Season with salt and pepper.

Fry the perch fillets for just 1 minute, skin down, in a non-stick pan with hot, frothy butter (they should remain soft).

Serve the fillets with the sauce and the lemon salt.

Wine pairing: Condrieu 2005 (Domaine Vallet)

Lake-Caught Crayfish, Corn Juice and Coriander

Serves 4

1 kg lake crayfish or
    langoustines
2 litres vegetable
    court-bouillon
1 tablespoon olive oil
5 cl Noilly-Prat
1 gelatine sheet
5 ears corn
30 cl milk
20 cl whipping cream
1 bunch coriander
salt and pepper

For the garnish
1 diced carrot
1 diced shallot
2 chopped tomatoes

Prepare the crayfish: completely gut the fish and cook them in a court-bouillon for 1 minute. Cool them down in the water by adding ice cubes. Remove the tails and claws (keep the shells). Place them in the refrigerator.

Prepare the jelly: in a saucepan, fry the shells in olive oil. Add the garnish, deglaze with the Noilly Prat, then add 30 cl of water. Simmer for 1 hour with the lid on.

Season with salt and pepper, then strain. You should obtain approximately 20 cl of liquid. Add the gelatine sheet. Divide the jelly into small glasses and place in the refrigerator.

Prepare the corn emulsion: simmer the ears of corn in milk for 30 minutes. Drain them and scrape off the kernels. Mash them through a sieve.

Leave to cool, then add the whipping cream. Season.

Just before serving: sauté the crayfish in a non-stick pan to warm them. Place them on the jelly, then cover with the corn emulsion, which you should first stir again to fluff it up: only take the top portion (you can also put the corn preparation into a cream siphon).

Sprinkle with chopped coriander and a few grains of salt.

Wine pairing: Pouilly-Fumé Buisson Renard 2004
(Domaine Didier Dagueneau)

Garden Herbs, Warm Vegetable Millefeuille and Chanterelle Pickles

Serves 6

1 kg large, firm-fleshed
    potatoes
1 kg carrots
300 g spinach
1 kg wild mushrooms
    (chanterelles, ceps,
    mousseron, pieds de
    mouton, etc.)
garden herbs: flat-leaf parsley,
    chives, tarragon
50 g pickled chanterelles
butter
sea salt

For the vinaigrette
vinegar
olive oil
grapeseed oil
salt
1 sugar cube rubbed
    with orange

Use a mandolin to thinly slice the potatoes and carrots. Steam the slices: the potatoes should be well cooked and the carrots very soft. Blanch the spinach and season it.

In a pan, fry the mushrooms in the butter for several minutes. Season and then chop them.

On a rectangular dish, stack alternating layers of potatoes, carrots, mushrooms and spinach. Place them under a press for 6 hours, then cut the millefeuille into rectangles.

Prepare the vinaigrette by mixing the ingredients. Just before serving, steam the millefeuille to warm it up. Serve warm with the vinaigrette, garnished with a few pickled chanterelles and garden herbs.

The millefeuille can be prepared using the same method with seasonal vegetables, and is the perfect complement to fish or meat. It was created for the Meilleur Ouvrier de France *competition in Toulouse in 2004.*

Wine pairing: Brèze 2002 White Saumur (Domaine Foucault)

Veal Sweetbreads, Rue and Raffia Potatoes

Serves 4

4 plump veal sweetbreads
30 g veal breast pieces
2 tablespoons oil
1 carrot
1 shallot
1 bouquet garni
½ clove garlic
30 g butter
1 teaspoon caster sugar
10 cl port
¼ litre white veal
    or poultry stock
2 large potatoes
1 litre oil
1 bunch rue
salt, pepper

raffia

Clean and peel the veal sweetbreads, then soak in fresh water with ice. Place them in a saucepan, cover entirely with water and blanch for 1 minute in simmering water. Drain and set aside in a cloth.

For the stock: in a cast-iron casserole dish, brown the pieces of veal breast in oil. Add the seasoning mixture (carrot, shallot, bouquet garni, garlic), then a pat of butter and the sugar. Caramelize. Deglaze with the port and cover with the veal stock. Simmer for 30 minutes. Strain, then simmer over low heat to reduce by one-quarter.

For the raffia potatoes: cut the potatoes into thin strips, then tie them with a piece of raffia blanched for 10 to 15 seconds in boiling water. Dip quickly in a hot deep-fryer, then season to taste.

Season the veal sweetbreads. Fry them in a pan with the remaining butter until nicely browned. Finish cooking them in an oven at 150°C for 7 to 8 minutes, basting lightly with the juices to make them glossy.

Before serving, steep the rue in the juice for 1 minute.
Season to taste and strain.

Serve the sweetbreads and the raffia potatoes with the juice on the side.

Wine pairing: Cuvée Confidentiel 2005 Mondeuse (Charles Trosset)

Barbotine-Cooked Country Potatoes

Serves 4

10 g salt
10 potatoes (Charlotte),
    40-50 g each
250 g kaolin clay
    (pure clay for ceramics)

Wash but do not peel the potatoes.

In a casserole dish, add 50 cl of cold water and the salt to the kaolin clay. Drop in the potatoes and bring to the boil. Place the entire dish in the oven and bake with the lid on at 150°C for 45 minutes.

Remove the potatoes using a long fork. Place them on a pastry rack, then reduce the oven heat to 90°C and bake for another 20 minutes to finish cooking.

Serve the potatoes with a zabaglione or as a side with fish, head of veal, etc.

Wine pairing: Pied de la Barme 2005 Mondeuse (Domaine Saint-Germain)

Pea Zabaglione, Serac Soup and Dried Alpine Beef

Serves 6

400 g shelled peas
1 tablespoon whipped cream
100 g dried beef (Grisons)
4 egg yolks
20 cl vegetable stock
nutmeg
100 g clarified butter*
sea salt
250 g serac
10 cl milk

Prepare the sides: boil the peas (3 to 5 minutes in a large pan of salted, boiling water). Mash half of them through a strainer. Add the whipped cream to this purée and season. Set aside to keep warm.

Dice the dried beef.

For the serac soup: blend the serac with the milk. You can add more milk if the mixture seems too thick. Season.

Prepare the zabaglione just before serving: emulsify the egg yolks with the vegetable stock, as for a hollandaise sauce. Add a bit of grated nutmeg and the clarified butter. Season.

Serve dishes of the zabaglione sprinkled with diced beef, warm peas, a few coarse grains of salt and freshly ground pepper. Set the cold soup and the warm pea purée on the side.

Wine pairing: Vin de Savoie Gringet Le Feu 2005 (Domaine Belluard)

Asparagus Tart, Sweet Almond and Egg Yolk

Serves 6

1 kg large green asparagus

For the hazelnut mixture
200 g butter
80 g caster sugar
10 g salt
200 g flour
50 g ground almonds
50 g ground hazelnuts
4 eggs

For the vinaigrette
50 g salt
55 g sugar
10 cl spirit vinegar
8 cl balsamic vinegar
13 cl olive oil
21 cl peanut oil

1 egg yolk

For the hazelnut mixture: mix the creamed butter* with the sugar, salt, flour, ground almonds and ground hazelnuts, then add the eggs one by one. Set aside at room temperature.

Peel the asparagus and cook for 7 minutes in salted, boiling water. Cool the asparagus, then cut in half lengthwise.

Arrange the asparagus in a ring or tart tin, head to tail. Cover with a thin layer of hazelnut mixture, then refrigerate for 1 hour.

Bake in a hot oven (250°C) for approximately 6 minutes.

Make the vinaigrette by mixing the ingredients. Flip the tart over, slice it into 5-cm-wide strips, then serve with the vinaigrette and raw egg yolk on the side.

Wine pairing: 1996 Château Simone Palette white

Beaufort Shortbread Biscuits, Dandelion Cones and Parmesan Marshmallow

For the Beaufort shortbread biscuits

Serves 8

200 g butter
200 g flour
200 g grated Beaufort
1 pinch salt

Mix all the ingredients to obtain a dough with an even, creamy consistency.

Form the dough into a roll and let it firm up in the refrigerator.

Cut the roll into 1-cm-thick circles.

Bake in a 200°C oven for 5 to 6 minutes.

Wine pairing: Roussette de Savoie 2005 (Domaine Blard)

For the dandelion cones

Serves 8

200 g butter
200 g caster sugar
20 g salt
200 g flour
100 g dandelion
hazelnut oil

Use an electric mixer to cream the butter* with the sugar, salt and flour.

Spread out the mixture on a baking sheet using a spatula, forming a thin, round layer. Bake at 180/200°C until the dough browns slightly. It should still be soft and malleable.

As soon as you take the dough out of the oven, form it into cones.

Cut up the dandelions, season with hazelnut oil and serve with the cones.

For the parmesan marshmallow

Serves 8

40 cl milk
60 g parmesan
3 g agar
2 egg whites

Boil the milk with 30 g of parmesan and the agar for 1 minute. Strain and leave to cool. Before the agar sets (after a few minutes), add the egg whites, which you should have beaten until they form stiff peaks.
Pour into a 2-cm-deep tin or mould, and refrigerate.

Before serving, cut into cubes and roll in the remainder of the grated parmesan.

Cherries, Elder Flower and Saint-Genix Biscuits

Serves 4

300 g cherries
1 bunch elder flowers
50 g caster sugar

For the praline biscuits
125 g caster sugar
2 eggs
125 g flour
3 g yeast
10 cl whipping cream
3 Saint-Genix pralines

1 piece gauze

Pit the cherries. Combine them with 50 g of sugar and soak for 1 hour.

Wrap the elder flowers in gauze. Cook the cherries and elder flowers together in 5 cl of water for 10 minutes, with the lid on. Leave to cool without removing the lid.

Press the gauze bag to extract the flavour from the flowers, then remove it. Set aside in the refrigerator.

Make the praline biscuit dough: cut the pralines into pieces and combine them with the remaining ingredients. Pour into a mould and bake at 180°C for 7 minutes.

Serve warm with the cherries.

Elder
Flower
Syrup

Makes 2 litres of syrup

400 g caster sugar
300 g elder flower heads
   (in full bloom)

Make a syrup with 2 litres of water and the sugar by letting the mixture boil for 1 minute. Pour the boiling syrup over the flowers, then simmer over the heat for 1 additional minute, lid on. Leave to cool.

Enjoy this syrup as a cold beverage. Its flavour is unparalleled, like a flavoured Cottat Sancerre.

Alpine Ice Cream, Meringue and Rhubarb

Serves 6

5 stalks rhubarb
50 g caster sugar

For the meringue
4 egg whites
    (approx. 100 g)
100 g caster sugar
100 g icing sugar

For the ice cream
25 cl milk
25 cl cream
40 g caster sugar

ice cream maker

Prepare the meringue: beat the egg whites with the caster sugar until they form stiff peaks, then fold in the icing sugar with a spatula.

On a 20-cm-long by 4-cm-wide sheet of Rhodoid or waxed paper, spread out the meringue in a stainless steel ring or a ramekin, then roll up the paper to form a circle. Leave to dry in a warm oven (70°C) for 1 or 2 hours, then remove the paper.

Cut the rhubarb into pieces and combine with 50 g of sugar (used solely to help the rhubarb drain before cooking). Stew in a saucepan for 20 minutes.

Prepare the ice cream: combine the cold milk with the cream and sugar. Leave the ice cream set in an ice cream maker (this step should be performed at the last minute).

Place a layer of rhubarb compote in the bottom of the meringue circle, then cover with ice cream.

Wine pairing: Coteaux de l'Aubance 2001 (Domaine Lebreton)

As the wind blows

Summer has finally returned, bringing something sweet and vibrant to the air. A gentle breeze blows across the colourful pastures, which in places are being harvested as hay, a vital resource with an incomparable fragrance. A few clouds float lazily across the sky, then mass together and disappear, chased away by the wind spirits.

Predator birds parade across the clear sky on the hunt, a silent procession of parasailers and hang-gliders. Always unpredictable, the mountain warms itself under the noon sun after the storm that raged there early this morning. Fog could return to blanket the landscape again before the day is out, and even now, a surprise snowfall could descend.

Life in the mountain pastures is getting organized. High-altitude farms and cottages have been reopened here and there. After the snowmelt, everyone has repaired roofs, stones and pathways. The livestock has been moved for the season. The villages have celebrated the cattle and sheep passing through, not to return to lower ground until September 15 or 20.

One of the many paths leading out of the valley along the torrents and waterfalls emerges onto the potholed country road that leads to the farm owned by Joseph's parents. The farmhouse is called 'Les Vieilles'. The altitude is displayed on the engraved wood of the facade: 1,670 metres. Lassie, the brave and valiant old dog, is splayed out on the ground whimpering. Joseph is brushing the pads of her feet, which were hurt during transhumance, with arnica. The other sheepdogs are nearby, barking.
Joseph's father stands in the doorway to greet Emmanuel.

For a chef, summer is the time to cook with alpine milk.
Joseph gives the grand tour: "There aren't very many farms like this that are still running. This pasture was redone fifty years ago, when it already belonged to my grandparents. They used to ride horses down, now we take the 4x4! ... Anyway, cheers!"

In the common room, everyone gathers around the table with its red-and-white-checked oilcloth covering. Joseph has already set out some small Savoie glasses made of coloured ceramic - and an old lemonade bottle full of booze!

On top of a tall bookcase, a wooden statue of the Virgin Mary and an arrangement of dried flowers and plants watch over the household. Soup heats over a wood-burning stove near the window while the group reminisces about a wedding that still holds special memories to the people of Megève. Emmanuel did the catering under a circus tent erected over the village skating rink. Joseph, who had been pressed into service as a 'protocol officer' for the occasion, drove the sleigh carrying the beaming newlyweds to the church.

"What time do you milk the cows?" asks Emmanuel.
"Around three or half past!"

Joseph laughs all the time, with a hearty, ringing laugh.

"The last time I came to get milk, it was with Michel Rostang!"

"I remember, your wife and the little ones were here!"

"Yeah, I'll have to come back with Clément and the girls."

"Absolutely! We had a lovely snack together."

"They were adorable!" remembers Joseph's mother, sitting slightly aside in the shadows.

Judith, her granddaughter, has come to sit on her lap and listen to the visitors.

Judith is fourteen. She has grown up between the village farm and the mountain pastures, staying with her grandparents on Wednesdays and for part of her school holidays. By now, she's become a big help to her uncle Joseph in milking the cows.

"And the other pasture is even higher up, isn't it? Do you stay there sometimes?" asks Emmanuel.

"Yes, there's an apartment over the stable! It's easier to get there. It's at more than 1,800 metres altitude, but the path is wider, and it doesn't have so many potholes!"

"What about when you're here, who comes to get your milk?"

"The *Cave des Saisies*. It's just at the edge of the village, at the cheesemaker's. But it's me who takes the milk down every day at 5.30 a.m. I get up at 4 to be down there by 6. They use my milk to make Beaufort, Reblochon, Savoie tomme and Abondance."

It's almost time for the milking. Emmanuel wants to milk the cows by hand, but they're not used to it anymore.

"Alright, let's go find them and then get started!" Joseph proclaims, looking at the clock.

Judith follows suit, pulling on her boots and work clothes. She takes two of the dogs and heads toward the top of the field, up to the edge of the pine trees.

One of the dogs, although impatient to work, is still too young and isn't allowed to follow her.

Joseph's father, staff in hand, watches his granddaughter as she quickly reaches the highest part of the prairie. The piercing clang of the cowbells, which are said to ward off vipers, echoes well beyond the edge of the forest. The herd of forty-odd cows moves ponderously down the hill and docilely enters the stable for the afternoon milking.

Everyone jumps quickly into the action. Emmanuel savours a glass of warm, foamy milk. The milking continues and the extracted milk goes directly to the canisters that have been securely attached to the 4x4.

Now the cows can leave the shed and return to their quiet grazing. The weather is hot. Joseph is going down into the valley once again; he knows every dip and bump in the steep road so well that he could almost drive it with his eyes closed.

"What does the weather say? When a storm hits here, it really hits hard! I have to hurry!"

"How are we going to get back down? Oh no, it's going to be worse going down than coming up!" jokes Emmanuel.

Before heading back to his car, Emmanuel leans over a dip in the road, at the edge of the woods.

"Look at that, it's a Lady's Slipper orchid! It's an incredible plant, a very rare orchid!"

"What are you going to do with it?" Judith wants to know.

"You don't do anything with it; you just look at it, that's all! It's smiling just for you to enjoy. When a flower becomes a legend, you don't want to pick it anymore."

As we leave the heights, it seems that the spirit of the mountain is watching over this serene corner of nature, despite the demons that still lurk. It protects the plants and the flowers and guards the mines and crystal caves too. Although it calls down tempests, it only does so to preserve the springs and fountains. Villagers try to attract it by planting elder trees, whose flowers can be used to preserve apples for a long time.

In the valley, the air is heavy, and the clouds are gathering. People say that there's soul in the air. Emmanuel has stopped in front of the *Feu-Follet* cottage at the edge of the village to check up on the Rucher de Champlat apiary and its owner, an unconventional beekeeper.

"You should have told me, I would have shaved! Here I am all dirty and, really, I would have put on my Sunday best. And really... a beekeeper should wear all white... Ouch, bloody bees! When it's stormy, they get a little aggressive! Sometimes I have as many as twenty stings! And whatever you do, don't get in the way of their landing strip. It's a real danger over on that side, there!

I have thirty-five beehives. If I work with iron, they get all worked up. They hate it when I do that! But they get along just fine with wood. They like wood. I'm pretty handy, and when I work with wood, it doesn't affect them at all!

Up here in the mountains, we make multi-flower honey, and I only harvest it once - just before 15th August. Beekeeping isn't the same here as it is in other places... one good hive can produce between twenty and forty kilos of honey a year."

"Will you call me when you harvest it?" asks Emmanuel.

"Up here in the mountains, we make multi-flower honey, and I only harvest it once - just before 15th August. Beekeeping isn't the same here as it is in other places... One good hive can produce between twenty and forty kilos of honey a year."

"That depends on my cousin. He's the one that has the extractor!" answers Christian, the beekeeper.

"Ow, bloody bees! Is my nose all red?"

Emmanuel has been stung.

"How many bees are there in a hive?"

"It depends on the queen," Christian continues.

He explains the matriarchal organization of a beehive. The queen is the only reproductive female surrounded by thirty to fifty thousand sterile worker bees, who make sure the hive runs smoothly. They switch jobs throughout their lifetimes, taking turns to play wet nurse, caretaker, storekeeper, guard, receiver, pollen-gatherer, etc.

"A good queen will give birth to thousands of bees! Theoretically, the queen lives for three or four years and the nectar flow lasts about twenty days... The nectar flow is when plant production of nectar is at its maximum. As soon as the nectar flow is over, the bees kill the drones, which are male bees that only exist to mate with the queen. Yes, you heard right: drones die after they make love! It's a cruel world. Bees don't do themselves any favours! When they get back to the hive, pollen gatherers transfer the nectar to another worker, who will in turn pass it to another, and so on until it reaches the storage cell. A bee that doesn't bring back any food doesn't get back into the hive. The guards kick it out and kill it!"

"Ow! Little sods! When they want to sting, they do it fast!" complains Emmanuel.

"Yeah, even though they know perfectly well that when they do, they lose their sting and die!"

The beekeeper explains that the bees are going up to higher altitudes less and less frequently; it depends on what's in bloom. They don't range any further than two miles from the hive. He adds that plant flowering is increasingly in jeopardy, and laments the fact that hay is being cut earlier and earlier. In the past, he continues, it took more than a month to cut the hay, and that was much better. People sowed oats, barley and sainfoin with its multitude of yellow and purple flowers.

"Here, we paint the beehives; it's prettier, and the bees can recognize their hive by its colour. But they can't see red! And look what happens if I move the purple hive and put it where the yellow hive should be..."

"Will it bother them?" wonders Emmanuel.

"They get confused. If you want to move a hive to a new location, you have to move it more than two miles away first, and leave it there for a fortnight. Afterward, you can put it back wherever you want, and the bees will find their way."

The beekeeper also explains that in order for honey to keep well, it mustn't contain too much water. That's why, when bees bring nectar in, they fan it and get rid of all the moisture through the flight hole. Maybe it's because of the mountain climate, or just because the beekeepers give the bees enough time to do their work, but the honey here never ferments. You can keep it for ten years.

"Our bees aren't afraid of the cold. They even go out in the winter, especially if the sun is out. In the mountains, our hives are double thickness, but it's not because of the cold - it's the humidity that they are really afraid of. The other day, I was talking to a beekeeper who told me that we work the way they do in Canada. Bees always go to the side with the daylight. They love it when neighbours hang laundry out to dry... But the neighbour might not appreciate the yellow marks on their clothes."

"Hold on, don't move! It's back!"

"Ah, another one! They're flying around because of the storm! Ok, it's on you now! They can't work the way they want to because of the electricity in the air, so... It went that way!"

"Oh! It's in my hair!" shouts Emmanuel.

Spring bees live for about two weeks, Christian explains. Later bees survive the winter because they work less. In August, they're still collecting pollen, but they store it for themselves. By the end of the harvest, beekeepers start to feed them as well. In the mountains, they can't survive the winter without someone taking care of them. Christian feeds them syrup, sugar candy or a bit of honey.

"Careful, here comes another one! Seeing the queen in the middle of the hive is almost impossible. One time, I made a hive with just one frame and I painted the queen red!"

"You painted the queen?" Emmanuel is amazed.

"Of course - with a paintbrush! But when I went to look for her, she wasn't there anymore! The hive had switched queens to form a new swarm. In a swarm, the old queen is always the one who leaves, with some scouts and workers. A travelling swarm isn't dangerous. The bees lose all of their defensive instincts if they don't have any territory to protect. I've been keeping bees for maybe thirty or forty years, but I'm no professional! I do it because I enjoy it... I know so many things that I can't explain..."

Emmanuel is expected in the kitchen.

"Well, Mr. Janin, if we don't see each other before then, tell me when you're going to harvest so I can come and see you."

"Sure, I'll let you know! I live just over there, a little farther down the road, across from... I stop in, I go back and forth, it forces me to walk! Sometimes, I collect a swarm here or there, in a loft or a tree somewhere. Eleven have already left this year... Ouch, bloody bees!"

Tomorrow, if the weather isn't beastly, as Emmanuel says, we'll go to see Thérèse. She opens the alpine chalet she inherited from her grandparents during the warm season. We'll eat omelettes made of Savoie meats, herbs and cheeses on the terrace overlooking the pasture, up above the bustling summer in the valley, to the sound of the accordion.

Caesar's Mushrooms, Pistachios **and** Parmesan

Serves 4

6 Caesar's mushrooms
30 g chopped pistachios
2 teaspoons pistachio oil
30 g parmesan
¼ lemon
sea salt
freshly ground pepper
8 parmesan marshmallows
  (see recipe page 113)

Slice the mushrooms thinly and lay them flat. Sprinkle each with a few grains of salt. Add one twist of freshly ground pepper, 3 drops of lemon juice, 1 stick of parmesan (1 to 2 mm thick), a few chopped pistachios and 1 drop of pistachio oil.

Prepare this dish at the last minute to keep the delicate woody flavour, the hint of fresh hazelnuts and almonds and the crunch.
Serve with parmesan marshmallow (see page 113).

Caesar's mushrooms (or Amanita caesarea) are pretty, bright orange mushrooms with white stems that are found in the south and in Italy. They can be eaten raw or cooked. Considered the king of mushrooms, they were once served only at the table of the Roman emperor, which is where their name comes from.

Wine pairing: Ermitage Grain d'or 2004 (Marie-Thérèse Chappaz)

Lightly Smoked Lake Trout, Hazelnuts and Marigold Sorbet

Serves 6

1 kg trout fillets (Lake Geneva)
90 g salt
10 g caster sugar

For the sorbet
1 large bunch marigolds
   (or tarragon)
200 g grapefruit flesh
25 cl orange juice
25 cl hazelnut oil

smoker
Pacojet (or sorbet maker)

Prepare to smoke the fish: combine the salt with the sugar and spread over the fish fillets. Refrigerate them for 3 hours.

Rinse the fillets and dry them using a cloth. Place them on the smoker and smoke them gently for 1 hour using spruce sawdust: the smoke should be very light to keep the trout soft and flavourful.

If you cannot smoke the trout fillets, cook them until just slightly warm and still pink.

For the sorbet: chop the marigolds (flowers and leaves) into large pieces. Warm up the orange juice and pour it over the marigolds. Leave to steep until cool, then strain.

Place the grapefruit flesh, the steeped orange juice and the hazelnut oil in the Pacojet bowl. Place in the freezer to set into sorbet.

Cut the trout fillets into ½-cm slices and arrange them on a dish.
Place them briefly in a salamander oven or under the grill. Serve immediately with a scoop of sorbet.

Marigolds are edible plants with yellow-orange flowers, in the same family as carnations. Their leaves release a fragrance of tarragon and grapefruit.

Wine pairing: Pernand-Vergelesses 1er Cru Sous-Frétille 2005
(Domaine Rapet)

Lamb Neck Confit, Herbs and Polenta

Serves 4

1 lamb neck (500-600 g)
50 g butter
50 cl collected lamb juices
10 cl white wine
1 clove garlic
1 carrot
1 onion
1 bouquet garni
1 tablespoon oil

For the polenta
100 g polenta
½ litre milk
3 sage leaves
1 bay leaf
1 sprig thyme
salt, pepper

2 tablespoons mustard
   (Savora)
100 g wild mushroom
   duxelles

For the lamb neck: bone the meat thoroughly, season it with salt and truss it.

Brown the meat in a casserole dish with the butter and oil. Add the garniture aromatique (the carrot and onion coarsely diced and the garlic clove), deglaze with white wine, then add the lamb juices.
Bake for 4 hours in a 150°C oven. Leave the meat to cool in the juices. Roll it up tightly in plastic wrap and refrigerate for at least 24 hours.

For the polenta: bring the milk to the boil. Season it, then steep the sage, bay leaf and thyme for about 3 minutes. Remove the spices, then gradually pour in the polenta. Cook for around 45 minutes, stirring frequently.

Pour the mixture into rectangular moulds (or ramekins) and place in the refrigerator.

Just before serving, slice the lamb and plate it with the polenta, warmed to room temperature and sprinkled with fresh chopped mushrooms and mustard.

Wine pairing: Crozes-Hermitage 2004 (Domaine Alain Graillot)

Risotto, Aromatic Herbs and Lemon

Serves 6

For the herb broth
1 stalk flat-leaf parsley
½ bunch tarragon
½ bunch coriander
300 g spinach
salt

1 finely chopped shallot
50 g butter
200 g Arborio rice
1 litre vegetable stock
50 g grated parmesan
30 g mascarpone
zest of 1 lime and 1 lemon
several drops lemon juice

For the herb broth: strip the leaves off the herbs and pull the stems off the spinach. Blanch them quickly in salted, boiling water, then cool down in ice water. Blend them and then mash through a sieve to obtain a smooth, tasty green purée. Set aside.

In a saucepan, sweat the chopped shallot with the butter. Add the rice and cook until transparent, stirring constantly. Once the rice has turned pearly, add enough vegetable stock to cover it. When the rice has absorbed all of the stock, cover it once again and repeat the process until the rice is completely cooked (15 to 20 minutes): cook the rice slowly, stirring regularly with a wood spatula.

Before serving, add the parmesan, mascarpone, herb broth, zest and lemon juice and season to taste.

Wine pairing: 2004 Château de Fieuzal white Pessac-Léognan

Beef and Herb Zabaglione

Serves 10

1.5 kg beef tenderloin
2.5 kg flank steak
10 cl grapeseed oil
2 sprigs thyme
2 bay leaves
pepper
3 juniper berries
3 cloves
15 thin bacon slices

5 egg yolks
10 cl vegetable stock
150 g clarified butter*
juice of ½ lemon
2 tablespoons chopped herbs
    (chives, tarragon,
    parsley, watercress)
salt, pepper
butter

The day before, begin marinating the beef flank steak and fillet with the oil and herbs.

On the day, wrap the beef fillet in the flank steak and roll it up tightly in a dishcloth. Refrigerate for 2 hours.

Next, cover the beef filet with the strips of bacon. Tie carefully and roast quickly, until nicely browned (approximately 4-5 minutes). Set the entire piece of meat aside in a cloth in the refrigerator.

Make the zabaglione: beat the egg yolks with the vegetable stock. Add the clarified butter, the chopped herbs and the lemon juice. Season to taste.Cut tournedos from the beef fillet. Cook them in butter, taking care that they stay rare. Serve with the herb zabaglione.

As a side dish, try French fries, polenta or potato puffs.

Wine pairing: Vin de Pays du Gard Clos de la Belle 2003
(Domaine Rémi Pedréno)

Blueberry and Wormwood Ice Cream Bars

Makes about fifty ice cream bars

4 egg yolks
30 g wormwood
250 g whipped cream
150 g white chocolate
100 g cocoa butter

For the syrup
80 g caster sugar

**For the blueberry
ice cream bars**
300 g blueberries (Jaillet)

ice-lolly moulds
fifty ice-lolly sticks

Make the syrup: bring 80 cl of water to the boil with the sugar. Leave to cool.

For the wormwood ice cream bars: pour half of the syrup over the yolks and cook like a zabaglione, beating until completely cooled. Add the wormwood and whipped cream. Pour into ice-lolly moulds, add sticks and place in the freezer.

Once the ice cream bars are frozen, heat the cocoa butter with the white chocolate. Remove the bars from their moulds and dip them in the chocolate. Set aside in the freezer.

For the blueberry ice cream bars: make a coulis with the blueberries and the remaining half of the syrup.

Stir together and mash through a strainer. Pour into ice-lolly moulds, add sticks and place in the freezer.

Petite Arvine Sorbet with Yo-Yo Biscuits

Serves 6

Syrup (55.5 g caster sugar
     + 45 cl water)
30 cl Petite Arvine
     (syrupy white wine)

For the biscuits
150 g flour
80 g butter
40 g caster sugar
40 g icing sugar
1 egg yolk
1 pinch salt
zest of 1 lemon

Pacojet (or sorbet maker)

For the syrup: in a saucepan, bring the water-sugar mixture to a boil and cook until it forms a syrup.

For the sorbet: combine the syrup with the wine. Check the sugar content and adjust if necessary, then pour into the sorbet maker to set in the freezer.

For the biscuits: combine all of the ingredients as though for shortcrust pastry. Roll the dough out very thinly and leave to rest in the refrigerator.
Use a pastry cutter to cut out biscuits in whatever shape you choose (pine trees, flowers, stars, etc.). Bake in a 180°C oven for about twenty minutes, until the biscuits are browned.

Sprinkle the biscuits with icing sugar and serve with the Petite Arvine sorbet.

Wine pairing: Petite Arvine du Valais Château Lichten 2004
(Maison Rouvinez)

Wild Strawberries, Vacherin and Coffee Tiramisu

Serves 6

2 egg yolks
50 g caster sugar
200 g whipped cream
200 g mascarpone
1 vanilla pod
2 espressos

200 g wild strawberries
100 g wild strawberry coulis
coffee and cocoa powder

For the biscuit
3 egg whites
100 g hazelnut flour
 (or ground hazelnuts)
100 g icing sugar
30 g caster sugar
2 coffees

For the meringue
4 small egg whites
 (approx. 100 g)
100 g caster sugar
100 g icing sugar

1 piping bag

For the biscuit: beat the egg whites with the caster sugar until they form stiff peaks. Add the hazelnut flour and icing sugar, stirring with a spatula. Spread the mixture out on a buttered sheet of greaseproof paper, then bake for 5 minutes at 180°C.

For the meringue: beat the egg whites with the caster sugar until they form stiff peaks, then add the icing sugar. Using a piping bag, form tubes on a buttered and floured sheet of greaseproof paper, then bake for 40 minutes in an 80°C oven (be careful: they're very fragile).

Beat the egg yolks with the 50 g of sugar to form a zabaglione. Mix the whipped cream with the mascarpone and the seeds from the vanilla pod. Combine the two mixtures, then separate into two portions and add the espresso to one.

Pour part of the coffee mixture into small square moulds and place in the freezer.

To assemble: spread out a layer of vanilla mascarpone in the bottom of a glass, cover with a few wild strawberries and top with the coulis, then place the coffee-infused biscuit on the plate. Add wild strawberries and the coffee mascarpone until the glass is full. Set aside in the refrigerator.

Just before serving, sprinkle with powdered coffee and cocoa. Present with a cube of frozen coffee mascarpone, a few wild strawberries and the meringues.

Wine pairing: Rivesaltes 1995 Château la Casenove (Etienne Montès)

Jellied Strawberry Juice with Evergreen Celery

1 kg strawberries
80 g caster sugar
12 sheets gelatine
5 lovage leaves

Remove the stems from the strawberries and cut the fruit into pieces. Weigh out 800 g of strawberries and cover with sugar to drain for 1 hour. Blend them in a food processor, then bring the resulting coulis to a boil. Once it reaches the boil, check the sugar content and add the gelatine, previously softened in a little cold water. Strain the mixture and pour the jelly out onto a baking sheet covered with plastic wrap. Leave to set in the refrigerator.

Once the jelly has set, arrange small piles of diced strawberries on top with chopped celery, then fold the jelly over them and cut out ravioli using a pastry cutter.

Serve quickly.

Wine pairing: FRV 100 Rosé Pétillant du Beaujolais
(Domaine Jean-Paul Brun)

Granita **and** Arbin Mondeuse

Serves 10

1 litre Arbin Mondeuse
    (or Syrah)
zest of ½ orange
¼ stick cinnamon
4 cloves
15 sugar cubes
1 vanilla pod, cut in half
1 star anise
10 juniper berries
2 tablespoons honey

Combine all of the ingredients with the wine. Bring to the boil and cook for 1 to 2 minutes. Strain the mixture and place it in the freezer.

Once the granita is frozen, break it into crystals using a fork and serve immediately.

Serve as a refreshing snack on a hot day, accompanied with biscuits.

Wine pairing: Arbin La Brova 2004 Mondeuse (Domaine Louis Magnin)

Spring Water in Spiced Jam

1 litre spring water
750 g caster sugar
55 g apple pectin (Vitpris)
150 g glucose

10 juniper berries
5 pine buds (optional)
5 cloves
1 star anise
1 vanilla pod
1 teaspoon Szechwan pepper
1 stick cinnamon

pastry thermometer

Combine the spices in a container. Pour the boiling spring water over them and leave to steep, covered, until cool.

Strain. Add 50 g of sugar and the pectin, then bring to a boil. Add the remaining sugar and the glucose.
Take care to skim regularly while cooking. Heat to 105°C (you can stop cooking when the mixture coats the back of the spoon), then pour into jars.

This jam goes perfectly with terrines of game and foie gras.

Barley Sugar **with** Mountain Flavours

500 g coarse granulated sugar
2 drops lemon juice
flavourings:
    juniper, pine, wormwood
food colourings:
    green, yellow, black

In a saucepan, bring 25 cl of water to a boil with the sugar. Pour the resulting syrup onto a marble slab or pastry mat. Flavour according to taste, add the food colouring and then work the sugar by hand, stretching it out to make it lighter, malleable and glossy. Cut it into hard candies or barley sugar sticks.

Wine pairing: Jurançon Ballet d'Octobre 2004 (Domaine Cauhapé)

The salt of the earth

Day has just begun to break, bathing the valley in a reddish glow and it's drizzling over the village.
This morning, the chef has decided to go hunting for mushrooms!
"We've already collected more than 100 kilos this year.
We haven't gone out many times, but every time we do, we find a lot!"

Over a cup of coffee in the kitchen, he laces up his boots. Nadine, his sous-chef, has collected the baskets and walking sticks. Every autumn, the chef brings the whole troop out to pick mushrooms.

The old Land Rover pulls up in front of the bakery.
"I know a spot, you'll see, it's like mushroom heaven! But first, pains au chocolat for everyone!"

At the edge of the forest, the fog barely muffles the sound of the troop's bells. Twigs snap with every step. They follow their noses, drunk on the rich smell of humus, in search of the promised bounty from the earth. Emmanuel often tromps along the sloping prairies and through the forest.
He's in his element!
Not far away, a tiny chalet appears at the edge of a clearing. He tells us that one day when he came here with his children to show them round death caps, the girls wanted to know who lived there. He told them that an old lady lived there alone, in the middle of the forest - when she suddenly appeared in the doorway and found the three of them, hands full of ceps.
"Uh, I was just showing my children the mushrooms!
"Kids are always a good excuse, aren't they!"

Petrified, Mathilde and Yoyo waited until the old woman had gone back inside to say, "That's the witch's house, isn't it, daddy?"
Emmanuel heads deeper into the woods.
"Anytime you see death caps, there are ceps nearby, either in the woods or else under the conifers, and also along the edge of the prairie. Just look at this boletus, what a beauty! A picture-perfect boletus protected from the light and the sun, what a find! And look at those! You don't find them like that often, not so close together. There could be twenty perfect ceps in the same place! They're all good ones, beautiful! This is a dream come true! It makes your eyes sparkle; all your cares float away! What if we put them straight into pastry, they'd be great, wouldn't they?
Now, what about that one? It smells like almonds. Watch out, that's a bad one, it's poisonous! The miller, on the other hand, is great - it smells like flour! Just like being in a flour mill. Nadine, have I had you smell the millers yet? I'll try to find you one. Here you go, stick your nose into that! Can you smell the difference? If you make a mistake, it'll cost you a serious case of the runs. But you won't die from it!"

Emmanuel deploys his troops. Nadine is close by, in charge of the baskets. He comes back after a while, grinning from ear to ear and holding out some pheasant's back mushrooms, which are eaten like ceps. "We'll have to look up the scientific name in the guide." The parasol mushrooms are a bit tired, but he'll dry those. There are a few saffron milk caps. He's prepared them in oil before; their orange colour stands out so well.

Nadine picks some heather to decorate the cep puff pastries. It's surrounded by blueberry brambles. "We used to pick blueberries with a comb, but it's not allowed anymore. When we get back, our hands are in a right state!" A little farther up, Emmanuel knows another place off the beaten track where there are very sweet blackberries as well. The harvest this year was exceptional. The climate plays into it: heat and rain both did their part.

The phone rings. "Hello, Monsieur Jacquier! I'm out mushroom-hunting! I'd love some perch, I'll take the same as on Wednesday... What about langoustines? People will want more for the holidays... Ones with large shells! No, I'm not much of a fan of clams! You know, this winter we should do some saltwater fish too. The iodine goes perfectly with mountain produce!"

The red morning sun continues to rise over the forest; it's time to head back for the lunch service.

There's not a bee in sight in front of the beekeeper's cottage!

The village is quietly preparing for autumn. Bad weather can arrive without any warning.

Emmanuel sits down at the table outside the restaurant to sort and clean the harvest while an apprentice stacks extra wood under the tent. Everyone's busy, from the front room to the cellar. In the kitchen, the pressure is rising. Emmanuel loves moments like this. He has put his collection of ceps, saffron milk caps and chanterelles into jars. A delivery person appears.

"Good morning, chef!" I've got a delivery for you.

"Oh, the Alba truffles! I was waiting for them. They're incredibly fragile, and they're best in November. I'll dampen them, scrub them and store them in rice. It keeps any moisture away and makes sure they don't touch each other!

Nadine, what's Daï working on?

I ordered three sacks of potatoes, and I only got three kilos!

Bernard, don't you have a dishcloth? Take two, that way you don't have to wipe your hands on your apron. Daï, we need to make a blancmange right away! No! Mushrooms! Floating Island!"

The phone rings again. Emmanuel asks his wife, Kristine, "How are the cats?", referring to his children, then turns to one of his chefs de partie: "Bernard is buying us all a round of drinks this evening. It's his birthday, and birthdays have to be celebrated!"

A spectacular cirque appears around a bend in the road. Grape vines cover it completely, along the top and down the slopes. Planted here through superhuman efforts, they now offer a view that resembles an ancient theatre whose tiers of seating have been overgrown.

The next day, Emmanuel goes to visit Marie-Thérèse Chappaz, on the other side of the mountain in Switzerland. This unusual vineyard owner has been defending the little-known vintages of her tiny Valais terroir for twenty years now. The two met at a tasting organized by the wine growers and chefs on the three sides of Mont-Blanc. "You'll see, she makes sensational wines! It's too bad I can't buy them for the restaurant. It's complicated - Switzerland isn't part of Europe."

Marie-Thérèse defines herself as a 'wine educator'. In Fully, it rains less than in Marseilles, as though a little Mediterranean enclave was hidden away in the heart of Switzerland. Her south-facing house is set on the hillside by a bend in the Rhône. It towers over the plain, which has always been covered with apricot orchards and fields of crops. Behind the house, the vines on the Liaudiziat estate run in terraced rows along the sunny slopes, dotted with almond and fig trees and herbs.

"We finished the grape harvest Saturday at five in the morning! The harvest is like the busiest rush of orders in a restaurant kitchen. Ah, I'm finally going to have time to come eat at your place, Emmanuel! We'll take a tour of the vines, but first, come here and let me make you a cup of coffee!"

Bounding happily, the Labrador leads the way. In the slightly bohemian house, paintings from artist friends sit alongside wine books and holiday souvenirs. The tiny, smiling blond woman loves to cook.

"So there's nothing left to harvest?" asks Emmanuel.

"No, it all happened very quickly! The fœhn blew through! And what about the mushrooms this year? There are a lot of them on your side, aren't there?"

"It was a good harvest thanks to the rain in August! I brought in more than 100 kilos!"

We have to take a cable-car to reach the vines, which climb as high as 650 metres. Slowly, the car glides upward. It stops halfway up the hill. "We wouldn't be able to harvest at all without this machine!" exclaims Marie-Thérèse.

The vineyard stretches along the nearby mountains between terraces formed of low, dry stone walls. This is where the winegrower lets her late varieties ripen. Everything is done by hand, from pruning to harvesting. As a disciple of farming methods that link the vineyard to the cosmos, she practices biodynamic agriculture.

"Those ones with a bit of grass in amongst them are my vines. I use plant-based treatments on them, like in homeopathic medicine. You have to help the vines resist threats using infusions. It's not easy, organic farming! It's not just a question of doing nothing and leaving the vines to fend for themselves!"

Emmanuel and Marie-Thérèse head toward the Combe d'Enfer. To get there, they have to cut through one of the many forests of chestnut trees that grow along the path connecting the hillside villages.

Because of the birds, large nets have been stretched out near the woods to protect the vineyard. This isn't just wine country; it's also chestnut country. In autumn, for the cantonal celebration, everyone gets together around a dish of brisolée, a local specialty made of roasted chestnuts served with bacon, cheese, nuts and grapes.

A spectacular cirque appears around a bend in the road. Grape vines cover it completely, along the top and down the slopes. Planted here through superhuman efforts, they now offer a view that resembles an ancient theatre whose tiers of seating have been overgrown. "There's never any wind at the Combe d'Enfer, and the summer is scorching! This land is ideal for growing grapes; it has a very unique composition, some granite, very little limestone."

Emmanuel slows down as they move through the trees.
"There aren't any truffles around here, with all the little oak trees?"
"Not that I know of. It's too dry," Marie-Thérèse responds.
"Anywhere there are grape vines, there are no mushrooms, but truffles really like vineyards!"
"Emmanuel, you seem to be something of a mushroom expert - where did you learn?"

In autumn, the merlot and cabernet sauvignon vines are the last to turn yellow. They stay green for a long time. Marie-Thérèse leans down to the bottom of the vine to pick a plump bunch of chasselas grapes. She holds it in her hands, which are as gnarled as a cep and stained by tannins from red wine.
"Look at the noble rot; it starts out as reddish spots, then it withers like an old woman's skin!"
On either side of the vines, wild thyme clings to the embankment. To increase the vineyard's longevity, Marie-Thérèse prunes her vines using a technique that resembles a corkscrew pattern.
"This vine dates back to 1886. The older they are, the better the grapes! You have to wait until the vine weakens a bit. Vines don't like being overfed. They're just like us: they need good food, but not too much!"
A little farther away, she also grows Marsanne, a variety similar to the Côtes-du-Rhône and Roussanne found in Provence. The Chasselas, Fendant and Petite Arvine vines stretch out like a range of yellow colour swatches.
Time to head back to the house for a tasting on the terrace, surrounded by fruit trees and overlooking the valley. Wine glasses and bottles await on the large, stone table.
Rather than a flattering Pinot, Marie-Thérèse prefers more unusual vintages: a white Humagne, a red Humagne, an Ermitage and a Syrah.
"Humagne is an old varietal from Valais. No one knows its exact origin. It's a slightly resinous vine."
We clink our glasses before tasting a very small production of the white Humagne, which improves with age. Emmanuel tastes it, swirls his glass, breathes in the aromas.

"It's not a fruity wine... and it doesn't have a mineral note either. It has hints of gentian; it's almost earthy."
"That's a 2004, this year's vintage will be better!"

At the beginning of the century, everyone in the region had their own little plot of Humagne vines and a wine press to make the infamous 'vin des accouchées' (wine for new mothers). Herbs would be added to a special goblet and then a good half-litre of the wine would be served in it to women in labour.

Marie-Thérèse produces seventeen different wines. She is proud of her Ermitage, an excellent wine to pair with poultry and almost any cheese. It's opulent, full-bodied. Some years, it contains hints of white truffle or raspberry brandy.
"The bouquet is really something! There's a note of herbs, a little dried apricot, maybe apricot stone?" ventures Emmanuel.

Winegrowers in the region have tended to harvest their grapes almost too quickly, without any sorting on the vine, and without taking sufficient advantage of the beautiful late autumn season.
"Should we 'aviner', rinse the glass with wine a little?" suggests Emmanuel.
"Actually, the term is enviner - everyone says it wrong! You rinse your glass to free the wine's aromas," corrects Marie-Thérèse. She was one of the first to make sweet wines with a long maturing process in the barrel, the sought-after syrupy varieties created with noble rot. "Everyone always wants sweet wine when they visit me, but I'd rather have you taste things that are different."

She serves a somewhat wild red wine with hints of gentian, earth and oak leaves. The oak bark is so strong that you can almost taste a note of cork.
"It's like the flavours of a Syrah, but less rich, less opulent, like some Mondeuses! It's very typical of the Aosta Valley, mellow but strong at the same time. This wine doesn't produce much sugar; it's not matured in barrels. You almost have to tame it. It's perfect with game. On the palate, it's very fluid at first. That's because the vines are young."
Emmanuel loves these unique, original and rare wines. He's a true connoisseur. He could spend all day discussing the depths and secrets of wine with Marie-Thérèse. He invites her to continue the conversation in Megève in a few days.

"Come eat at *Flocons* next week! You bring the wine, and I'll provide the truffles!"

Boar Meat Pie Sprinkled with Chicory Dust

Serves 4 to 6

1 wild boar shoulder
3 litres Mondeuse
    (Savoie red wine)
50 g caster sugar
5 cl cognac
2 litres game stock
salt, pepper
1 drop peanut oil
1 pat butter

For the garniture aromatique
1 bouquet garni
¼ orange
3 carrots
1 onion
1 clove garlic
juniper berries, cloves,
    peppercorns

For the mashed potatoes
400 g potatoes
    (such as Ratte)
5 cl milk
200 g butter

1 teaspoon chicory seeds
    and 1 teaspoon
    powdered chicory
a sprinkling of truffle flakes
    (optional)

Marinate the boar shoulder for 24 hours in the Mondeuse with the garniture aromatique cut into large, evenly-sized cubes.

Drain the meat and season it with salt and pepper. In a casserole dish, brown it on each side with the oil and butter, then add the garniture aromatique. Caramelize with the sugar and flambé in cognac.

Add the game stock and the wine from the marinade (boiled and strained first), then heat until it begins to simmer. Bake the casserole dish at 100°C for approximately 12 hours, with the lid on.

Decant, then shred the meat. Strain the remaining cooking juices. Reduce the juices, add the roasted chicory seeds, strain, then season to taste to obtain a rich, fragrant mixture. Add the meat.

For the mashed potatoes: cook the potatoes in water, with their skins on, for 20 minutes. Drain and peel them, mash them through a strainer, then add the milk and butter in small pieces to the warm potato. In a gratin dish or a stainless-steel ring, spread out a layer of shredded boar meat followed by a layer of mashed potatoes, top with reduced cooking juices, add the chicory powder and, if desired, a few truffle flakes. Serve immediately.

Wine pairing: Côte Rôtie 2001 (Domaine Jamet)

Caramelized Pork Belly and Onion Tart

Serves 4

500 g fatty pork belly from
    farm-raised pigs
50 g butter
1 bay leaf
1 sprig thyme
coarse salt, peppercorns
juniper
100 g Saint-Genix
    praline powder

For the onion tart
300 g small onions
50 g butter
30 g honey
juniper powder
100 g puff pastry
    (see recipe page 216)

vacuum machine

Season the pork belly (salt, pepper, juniper) and place it sous vide with 50 g of butter, the thyme and the bay leaves. Cook at 80°C for 16 hours.

Cut the pork belly into cubes (approximately 6 cm by 6 cm), sprinkle with praline powder and caramelize.

If you do not have a vacuum machine, you can braise the pork belly: cook it with braising* sauce, covered, in a 110°C oven for 6 hours.

For the onion tart: peel the onions and cut them in half. Steam cook them for about 15 minutes. Caramelize them with the honey and juniper powder, arrange them in a circle and cover them with a very thin sheet of puff pastry. Bake the tart like an upside-down tart in a very hot oven (250°C) for 4 to 5 minutes. Serve the tart with the pork belly.

Wine pairing: St Emilion Grand Cru 2002 Lafleur Vachon (Domaine Tapon)

Roast Pigeon, Blueberry Juice **and** Churros

Serves 4

4 pigeons
50 g butter
2 cl oil
200 g blueberries on braches
15 juniper berries cut
    in half

For the blueberry juice
10 cl vegetable stock
10 cl cream
10 cl milk
a few drops of
    wine vinegar
salt, pepper

For the churros
100 g butter
1 pinch salt
200 g flour
3 eggs
40 g aged tomme, grated
oil for frying

piping bag with star tip

Clean out and truss the pigeons. Then season the birds, brown them in a sauté pan with the oil and butter, then roast in the oven at 210°C for 7 to 8 minutes. Leave to rest in a covered casserole dish with the blueberry branches and the juniper berries.

For the blueberry juice: bring the vegetable stock to the boil with the cream and milk. Combine with the blueberries. Season to taste and strain. Finally, add a few drops of wine vinegar. Set aside.

Finish cooking the pigeons in the covered casserole dish for around 12 minutes, depending on their size.

For the churros: in a saucepan, bring 20 cl of water to the boil with the butter and salt. Remove from heat, add the dry flour (like a choux pastry), the eggs one by one, then the tomme. Leave the dough to rest for several minutes. Use a piping bag with a star tip to form churros, approximately 4 cm long each. Fry them for about 3 minutes in 180°C oil. Serve the pigeons with the blueberry juice and the browned churros.

Wine pairing: Faugères S 1996 Château des Estanilles

Cep Crystals

Makes approximately 50 pieces

200 g glucose
300 g fondant
500 g fresh ceps or
    50 g dried ceps
12 g butter
sea salt

1 baking sheet
pastry thermometer

For the crystals: cook the glucose with the fondant to 135°C. Pour the mixture onto a baking sheet to cool. Crush it into powder.

For the ceps: slice the ceps thinly and spread them out on racks. Dry them in a 50°C oven for 2 to 3 hours. Crush them to form a powder.

Combine 2 spoonfuls of crystals with 1 spoonful of dried ceps and ½ spoonful of salt.

Form them into the shape of mushrooms on the baking sheet. Bake in a 80°C oven for 2 to 3 minutes. Leave to cool.

You can use these ceps to garnish a dish or enjoy them with drinks.

Cep Puff Pastries

Serves 4

4 plump cep bouchons
150 g cooked foie gras
250 g puff pastry
    (see recipe page 216)
1 egg
salt, pepper

Clean and dry the ceps.

Wrap each cep in foie gras. Season with salt and pepper. Enclose each in puff pastry individually, then use a brush to glaze* the dough with the beaten egg mixed with a small quantity of water. Salt and set aside in the refrigerator.

Fifteen minutes before serving, bake in a 210°C oven until the pastry is well browned.

Wine pairing: Saumur-Champigny Les Poyeux 2002 (Clos Rougeard)

Wild Mushrooms
and Autumn Jars

500 g chanterelles
1 bay leaf
1 sprig thyme
20 cl olive oil
5 cl wine vinegar
1 tablespoon caster sugar
salt

For the "boutons de guêtres" chanterelles

Wash the chanterelles and dry them on a cloth.
Cook them for 2-3 minutes with the olive oil, vinegar, bay leaf, thyme, sugar and salt. Put them into jars, then seal and sterilize them.

To be enjoyed throughout the year.

1 kg saffron milk caps
several juniper berries
several peppercorns
1 bay leaf
grapeseed, hazelnut
**   or peanut oil**

For the saffron milk caps

Clean the mushrooms with vinegared water and dry them in a cloth. Put them into jars. Cover them with the oil of your choice and add herbs, avoiding any air bubbles that can speed up fermentation.

Use this method to store mushrooms for no more than a few weeks.

500 g morels
1 litre dry white wine
1 litre fruit brandy
2 cl Viandox®

For the morels

Wash, blanch and dry the morels, then pour the white wine, brandy and Viandox® over them.

This recipe can be used in preparing sauces or to deglaze juices.

Floating Island with Wild Mushrooms and Alba Truffle

Serves 4

4 eggs
1 Alba truffle (20 g)
400 g wild mushrooms
20 g butter
20 cl milk
10 cl cream
1 pinch salt
1 drop Viandox®
1 tablespoon hazelnut oil
1 shallot
salt, pepper

4 rings or ramekins,
    7.5 cm in diameter

The day before, place the whole eggs with the truffle so that they absorb its flavour.

On the day, clean the mushrooms and set aside the trimmings. Sweat them with 10 g of butter, add the milk and cream and bring to the boil. Mash together. Strain and season to taste.

Clarify the eggs (separate the whites from the yolks). Beat the whites until they form stiff peaks (but are not too firm) with a pinch of salt and 1 drop of Viandox®. Grease the rings and place them on waxed paper, fill them halfway with the egg white mixture, place a yolk in the centre and the remainder of the whites on top. Cook the floating islands on a low setting for several minutes in a steamer or rice maker. In a sauté pan, sweat the chopped shallot with the remaining butter. Add the mushrooms, then season to taste. Set aside to keep warm.

Remove the islands from their rings into a soup plate and garnish with the mushrooms, emulsified creamy broth and truffle flakes.

Wine pairing: Pouilly-Fuissé Tournant de Pouilly 2000 (Domaine Ferret)

Venison Backstrap, Liquorice and Root Vegetable Purée and Cumin-Cinnamon Potato Puffs

Serves 4

1 venison backstrap
40 cl balsamic vinegar
20 g butter
2 cl oil
salt, pepper

For the root vegetable purée
500 g parsnips
500 g Jerusalem artichokes
200 g Vitelotte potatoes
20 cl whipping cream
2 sticks liquorice or
    liquorice bites

For the potato puffs
2 kg potatoes
cumin powder
cinnamon powder
oil for frying
table salt

Bone the venison backstrap and slice into fillets. Set aside in the refrigerator.

For the liquorice and root vegetable purée: steam the vegetables separately (they must be very tender). Combine them and mash through a sieve, then drain the purées in a dishcloth. Boil the whipping cream with the liquorice, steep until the mixture has cooled, then strain. Combine with the root vegetable purée and season to taste.
Reduce the balsamic vinegar to obtain 10 cl.

For the potato puffs: form the potatoes into round or oval shapes and cut them into 3-mm-thick slices, then arrange them on a dishcloth to remove the moisture from them. Heat oil in a deep-fat fryer to 120-130°C, drop in a dozen slices and unstick them using a back-and-forth motion: after a few minutes, small bubbles should form. When they do, drop the potatoes into a second fryer with oil at 180°C (the temperature shock causes them to puff up). Do not let them brown; drain them and set aside in a cloth. Just before serving, drop the potatoes back into 170°C oil to brown, dry well, then sprinkle them with a salt/cumin/cinnamon mixture.

Season the venison fillets. In a sauté pan, brown them with the oil and butter on all sides, then set aside in aluminium foil.

At the last moment, finish cooking in a hot oven (180°C) for several minutes, making sure that the fillets remain very pink in the centre.
Arrange them on the plate with the reduced balsamic vinegar, the liquorice and root vegetable purée and the potato puffs.

Wine pairing: Gevrey-Chambertin 1er Cru Les Champeaux 2000 Denis Mortet

Chestnuts, Hay and Dried Beef

Serves 4

Puff pastry
Détrempe*:
160 g flour
25 g creamed butter
6 g salt

Beurre manié*:
160 g butter
60 g flour

Glaze*:
1 egg
salt

For the chestnut emulsion
150 chestnuts
100 g whipping cream

1 small teaspoon
	juniper powder
sea salt
diced dried beef
	(or Grisons beef)
truffle flakes
a few oven-roasted chestnuts

cream siphon
pastry thermometer

For the puff pastry: prepare the *détrempe* by mixing the flour and the creamed butter with 10 cl of water and the salt. For the *beurre manié*, combine the butter and the flour. Refrigerate for several minutes.

Spread out the *beurre manié* into a rectangle of dough. Do the same with the *détrempe*, which should be two-thirds the size of the *beurre manié*. Layer the two types of dough on top of one another and fold the rectangles according to the diagram on page 233. Note: both types of dough should have the same consistency.

Spread out the dough and form a double fold, again following the diagram on page 233. Refrigerate on a cloth for 20 minutes, then repeat the process: spread out the dough, form a double fold with a quarter fold. Refrigerate for another 20 minutes on a cloth. Form one more quarter fold, then a single fold, as in the diagram on page 233, adding half the juniper powder and the sea salt. Leave to rest for another 20 minutes in the refrigerator.

Spread out the dough to approximately 4 mm thick, then glaze using a brush (beaten egg + water + salt). Finally, sprinkle it with sea salt and the remaining juniper powder. Bake for 10 minutes in a 220°C oven, then reduce the heat to 120°C and continue baking for 30 minutes.

Make the chestnut emulsion: peel the chestnuts, cover with cold water and cook for 30 to 40 minutes. Mash them through a sieve. Add the whipping cream, heat the mixture to 60°C and put it in a cream siphon with one charger.

Once the dough is cooked, cut it carefully into rectangles or squares using a serrated knife. Serve with the garnishes (diced beef, truffle flakes and chestnuts) and the warm chestnut emulsion.

You can also use puff pastry* from your baker.

Wine pairing: White Clos des Papes 1996 Châteauneuf du Pape (Domaine Paul Avril)

Egg Yolk, Cassava Sticks and Coffee Oil

1 raw egg yolk (farmhouse)
2 cassava roots
2 litres milk
1 teaspoon clarified butter*
1 tablespoon sea salt
coffee oil

For the cassava sticks: cook the roots in milk over low heat for approximately 1 hour, then cut them into sticks. Brown them in clarified butter. Season with sea salt.

Dip the sticks in the egg yolk (separated from the white at the last moment) and the coffee oil.

This dish composed of simple, rustic ingredients is a match made in heaven. Virgin coffee oil is obtained from roasted Arabica coffee beans diluted with rapeseed oil.

Wine pairing: Clos des Grives 2005 white Crozes-Hermitage (Domaine Combier)

Polenta, Citrus Fruit and Green Anise

Serves 4

For the citrus compote
1 untreated lime
1 orange
15 cl orange juice
150 g caster sugar

For the ravioli
5 sheets gelatine
100 g caster sugar
20 cl lemon juice
green anise

For the polenta
50 cl orange juice
100 g polenta
1 pinch caster sugar
10 g butter

For the citrus compote: zest the lime. Dice the lime, blanch three times (see page 43), then cool. Cut the lemon into sections and cook with the orange juice, 100 g diced orange and the sugar for about 20 minutes. Once the mixture is cooked, mash and add the zest. Set aside in the refrigerator.

For the ravioli: soften the gelatine sheets in a little cold water. Bring 25 cl of water to a boil with the sugar, lemon juice and green anise. Remove from the heat and add the gelatine. Strain the juice, pour it onto a baking sheet, cover with plastic wrap and place in the refrigerator. Once the gelatine has set (after approx. 15 minutes), arrange the compote on top of it in small piles spaced 10 cm apart, then fold into the shape of ravioli. Use a knife to cut into rectangles. Set aside in the refrigerator.

For the polenta: cook the polenta (approx. 20 minutes) in the orange juice. Empty it out into a mould and set aside in the refrigerator. Just before serving, cut into rectangles and brown in a non-stick pan with a pat of butter and a pinch of sugar.

Serve the warm polenta sticks with the cold ravioli.

Wine pairing: Ruster-Beerenauslese 1995 (Domaine Landauer)

Hokkaido Squash, Hazelnuts and Mountain Honey

Serves 4

1 small Hokkaido squash
30 g caster sugar
1 vanilla pod
150 g whipped cream
5 cl liquid mountain honey

For the hazelnut cream
5 cl milk
10 cl whipping cream
5 cl hazelnut oil
(from Jean-Marc Montegottero at the Beaujeu oil mill)
20 g ground hazelnuts

cream siphon

Peel the squash and cut it into pieces. Cook for a few minutes in a casserole dish. Drain using a dishcloth, then mash through a strainer to obtain 200 g of pulp. Add the seeds from the vanilla pod, the sugar and the whipped cream. Divide the mixture into four glasses.

Cover with liquid honey.

Using a cream siphon, make the hazelnut cream by mixing the milk, cream and hazelnut oil. Screw in one charger and shake. Cover the honey with hazelnut cream and sprinkle with powder.

Wine pairing: Duval-Leroy Rosé de Saignée

Ugine Six-Hour Apples and Granny Smith Jelly

Serves 4

4 firm, locally-grown apples
   (that have never
   been refrigerated)
4 Granny Smith apples
200 g caster sugar
80 g butter
1 stick cinnamon
1 star anise
5 g apple pectin
1 drop natural green food
   colouring (optional)

For the caramel
200 g caster sugar

4 small sous vide
   cooking bags
vacuum machine
juice extractor

Peel the locally-grown apples but leave them whole. Run the Granny Smiths through a juice extractor.

Prepare the caramel: cook the sugar with 50 cl of water until the syrup turns brown. Stop cooking and add 70 cl of apple juice (watch for spattering). Leave to cool.

Into each bag, place 1 apple, 5 cl caramel, 20 g butter, 1 piece of cinnamon and ¼ star anise. Place the bags sous vide and cook at 80°C for 6 hours: the apple should become soft and take on the dark blond colour of the caramel.

Bring the remaining apple juice to a boil, add the pectin and 1 drop of green food colouring if necessary.

Serve the caramelized apple with the warm juice.

Wine pairing: Opulence sweet Vin de Savoie (Domaine Magnin)

Almond Tubes
with Cherries

Serves 4

150 g fondant
100 g glucose
80 g ground almonds
60 g butter
1 drop almond extract
50 g brandied cherries
50 cl whipping cream

pastry mat
baking sheet
cream siphon
pastry thermometer

Cook the fondant with the glucose to 150°C (hard crack stage). Remove from heat and add the ground almonds, butter and almond extract. Scoop out onto a pastry mat (Silpat) and let cool.

Grind the mixture to obtain a powder. On a baking sheet, form the powder into rectangles. Place in a 100°C oven and let melt for several minutes before rolling the rectangles around a tube. Leave to cool.

Make the cream: mix the whipping cream with the cherry juice. Pour into a cream siphon, then set aside in the refrigerator.
Just before serving, fill the tubes with cherry cream and garnish with the cherries.

Soufflée, **Local** Morello Cherries **and** Brandy

Serves 4

30 g creamed butter
30 g caster sugar
6 egg whites
300 g brandied
   Morello cherries

For the confectioner's custard
2 egg yolks
50 g caster sugar
15 g confectioner's cream
   powder (or flour)
20 cl milk

4 oven-safe dishes

Prepare the pastry cream: mix the egg yolks with the sugar and confectioner's cream powder until the mixture turns a pale yellow colour. Pour in the boiling milk. Put the entire mixture back into the saucepan and return to the boil, then cook for 3 minutes. Leave to cool.

Grease each dish with creamed butter using a brush and sprinkle with sugar.

Prepare the soufflé mixture: pour the confectioner's custard into a mixing bowl or stainless steel bowl. Add the egg whites, beaten until they form stiff peaks, by gently folding them in with a metal or rubber spatula. Add the pitted cherries. Pour the mixture into the dishes. Arrange several cherries on top and bake in a 200°C oven for approximately 8 minutes, depending on the size of the dishes.

The brandied cherries should have been prepared in the spring with 200 g Morello cherries, 20 cl fruit brandy, 150 g sugar and 1 cinnamon stick.

The Mountain

Emmanuel often talks of the one who lives far above the mountain pastures. A being full of vitality, with deep blue eyes that sometimes take on the colour of a joyous, crystal-clear sky.

You don't always see him when you go to visit. Sometimes he disappears with no explanation, but it's easy to predict when he's in a dark mood by the thick clouds drifting down into the valley. Besides, he doesn't place his trust in just anyone; he has to be coaxed.

Although he loves being near the sun, he has never seen the sea. They also say that he has never been married: he has far too much to do. Still, he has the tranquil air of those who walk and meditate. It goes together. And when he stands there in front of you, he has the strength of a lion. His voice sweeps stones and torrents from one valley to the next. He needs such a deep voice to cut through blizzards. Only the eagles and, lower down, the dogs and the cowbells answer back.

He is much quieter with people. He prefers to let them tell their stories around the fire, stories of genies and devils; to let them remember the wars, the pilgrims, the curious, the lost and the imprudent of every kind that he, too, has come across.

He watches fiercely over his kingdom of snow, full of hope and younger than ever. He - Mont-Blanc - is admired as much as feared...

Glossary

Beurre manié: French for "kneaded butter", a mixture of butter and flour used to make puff pastry.

Braising: cooking over low heat in a covered container.

Clarified butter: to obtain 50 g of clarified butter, melt 75 g of butter, then leave to rest for 10 minutes without stirring. The whey in the butter will sink to the bottom while the clarified butter floats to the surface, where it can be scooped out using a small ladle or a spoon.

Creamed butter: butter that has been worked until soft, taking on the consistency of an ointment.

Détrempe: mixture of flour, water and salt used to make puff pastry (see diagram).

Double fold: method of combining types of dough for puff pastry (see diagram).

Glaze: whole egg beaten with a little water that is spread over pastry to help it brown while baking.

Layering puff pastry dough: puff pastry is prepared in several phases (see diagram).

Monter au beurre: to improve the consistency of a warm sauce by whisking in small pieces of butter.

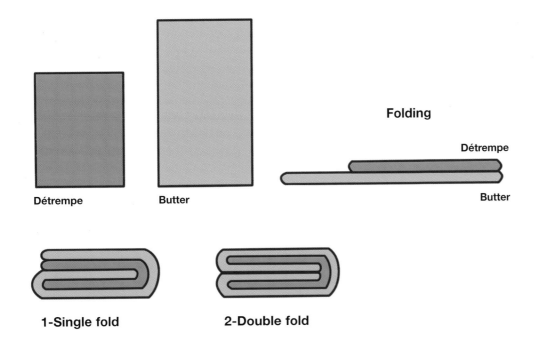

Détrempe

Butter

Folding

Détrempe

Butter

1-Single fold

2-Double fold

Acknowledgements

Emmanuel Renaut thanks his wife, Kristine.

Isabelle Hintzy would like to thank Emmanuel Renaut, who trusted her in developing
and completing this joint project.
She has been fortunate enough to follow his progress and enjoy his friendship for some ten years.
For Isabelle, Emmanuel's strict and demanding nature counterbalances his daring and creativity to create true
mountain cuisine. He has integrated into the village of Megève so well that he has become a native of the region.
Thank you to Nadine, who cooks with Emmanuel; and the entire highly-talented team
at *Les Flocons de Sel* and *Puck* restaurants.

Fondest wishes to Kristine, Mathilde, Johanna and Clément.

A warm thank you to the Megève tourism office for their kind, attentive support,
to its director Adrien Duvillard and to Marithé Crozet, director of communications.

Another warm thank you to Jean, the home distiller, in remembrance. Regrettably, Jean has passed away since
our winter visit. To Patrick and Gérard, who invited us to share their morning snack in Marcel's carpentry shop;
to baker Rémy Coste; to Joseph Socquet, the farmer in Megève and his entire family in their mountain cottage;
to Éric Jacquier and his wife Nathalie along Lake Geneva; Thomas from the cheese cooperative in the Vallée
des Arves; to beekeeper Christian Grosset-Janin; and to Marie-Thérèse Chappaz, wine educator in Fully.
Thank you as well to Thérèse of the high-mountain restaurant Le Sciozier and to Delphine of Terass Park
Hôtel for their help; to Catherine Navarro-Tissot for her *joie de vivre* et to Jean-Michel Deschamps
de la Prairie for his lovely autumn apples and his invaluable information. We would like to
thank the following companies for lending their tableware and decorative objects:

Angel des Montagnes
Alexandre Turpault
Bernardaud
Bougies La Française
Catherine Navarro Antiquités
Comptoir de Famille
Coucke
Cristal de Sèvres
Descombes Création
Clement

Sylvie Coquet for Feeling's
Ivv
Jars Céramiste
Le Jacquard Français
Loisirs & Création
Pierre Frey
Villeroy & Boch
Wmf
Yves Delorme

Graphic design and production: Élisabeth Ferté
English version (translation and page layout): I.D.O. Paris21

ISBN: 978-2-7006-0644-7

Photoengraving: Quadrilaser
© 2008, Aubanel, a brand belonging to Éditions Minerva, Geneva (Switzerland)
Printed in October 2008
By Kapp Lahure et Jombart printers in Evreux
Printed in France
Dépôt légal: November 2008

Visit www.editionsaubanel.fr